PRODUCTIVITY HACKS

500+ Easy Ways to Accomplish More at Work—
THAT ACTUALLY WORK!

Emily Price

Adams Media
New York   London   Toronto   Sydney   New Delhi

A **adams**media

Adams Media
An Imprint of Simon & Schuster, Inc.
57 Littlefield Street
Avon, Massachusetts 02322

First Adams Media trade paperback edition December 2018

ADAMS MEDIA and colophon are trademarks of Simon & Schuster.

For information about special discounts for bulk purchases, please contact Simon & Schuster Special Sales at 1-866-506-1949 or business@simonandschuster.com.

The Simon & Schuster Speakers Bureau can bring authors to your live event. For more information or to book an event contact the Simon & Schuster Speakers Bureau at 1-866-248-3049 or visit our website at www.simonspeakers.com.

Interior design by Katrina Machado

Manufactured in the United States of America

10 9 8 7 6 5 4 3 2 1

Library of Congress Cataloging-in-Publication Data has been applied for.

ISBN 978-1-5072-0960-8
ISBN 978-1-5072-0961-5 (ebook)

CONTENTS

INTRODUCTION

Trying to get a major project done but distracted by a growing list of smaller to-dos? Outsource.

Working from home but can't stay focused? Take a quick shower to boost concentration.

Ready to disconnect from the office but still getting work messages at eight p.m.? Get a separate work number.

Productivity Hacks is packed with more than 500 simple productivity-boosting hacks just like these, and more than twenty hack lists to help you become a productivity pro—or at least a little better at warding off procrastination. Broken up into chapters based on your needs, you'll find hacks on everything from productively working from home, to productive business travel, to holding office meetings that leave everyone energized and ready to work—instead of ready for a nap. You'll also find great online resources and apps for making the most of your time.

And productivity isn't just for work! Your personal life also requires organization and care—things that can easily get lost in the shuffle of a hectic workweek. *Productivity Hacks* has a chapter on striking that delicate balance between your work life and home life, so you can leave the office *at* the office.

With *Productivity Hacks*, there's advice for every get-it-done-now situation, so you can read the section where you need the most help or flip to any page for a quick fix. Wherever you need to get things done, we've got you covered, so let's start improving your productivity right now!

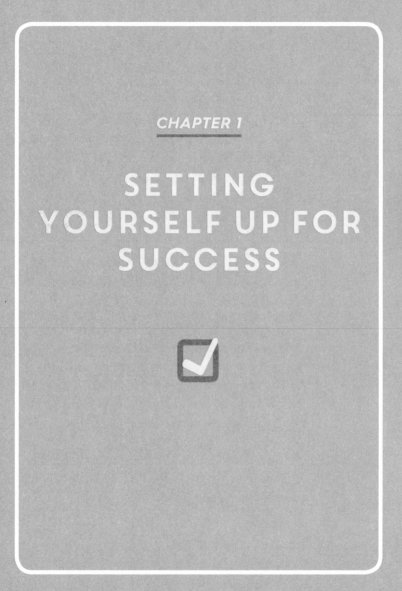

CHAPTER 1

SETTING YOURSELF UP FOR SUCCESS

1. **Plan your week on Sunday night.** You don't need to come up with a detailed hour-by-hour schedule, but spending a few minutes on the weekend planning what you hope to accomplish during the week can be a great way to set yourself up for success come Monday morning. Divide the responsibilities you have for the week onto specific days. This practice will give you a good idea of what your workweek will look like, and it will help you know whether or not you have time to take on additional projects.

2. **Prep, prep, prep.** Before you go to bed each night, set yourself up for success in the morning by prepping things you'll need when you wake up. This can be as simple as laying out your outfit for the next day and putting your workbag by the door, or as involved as planning out exactly what time you aim to do each part of your routine and grinding beans for your morning cup of joe. When you wake up groggy in the morning, you'll thank yourself for making things a little easier.

3. **Start the day with water.** Your first instinct in the morning might be to reach for a cup of coffee, but you're much better off if you reach for a glass of water instead. When you first wake up, you're often dehydrated because you spent the whole night not consuming any fluids. Add a cup of coffee on top of that, and you're actually becoming more dehydrated, thanks to the diuretic effect of all that much-needed caffeine—making it even harder for your body to get going. Kick things off with a big glass of water in the morning before making the switch to coffee—you'll feel refreshed and get your day off to a much better start.

4. **Eat breakfast.** You know how your mom always told you that breakfast is the most important meal of the day? She was right. Having break-fast jump-starts your metabolism and lets your body know that it's time to get things done. Beyond helping you wake up and ease into the day, a good breakfast will give you the energy you need to be productive in the morning, and it will help keep your mind off food until lunchtime.

5. **Keep your alarm clock away from the bed so you can't hit that snooze button.** You may think you're getting some much-needed extra sleep with those five more minutes in dreamland, but you're actually resetting yourself to the beginning of your sleep cycle, which means you'll be even more tired when you do get out of bed. Snoozing also takes time away that you could be using to handle your morning routine. Those minutes could be used for a quick breakfast that you usually don't have time for!

6. **Schedule a weekly or biweekly "maintenance day" where you say no to additional commitments and instead focus on tasks you need to finish for your home.** You can use this day to tidy up your home, pay bills, do laundry...anything you need to set yourself up to be successful. For instance, you might assign the first and last Sunday of the month as "maintenance days." When you know you have a maintenance day coming up, it's much easier to prioritize other commitments during the week without that stress about a home project.

7. **Create a visual "chain" of consistency.** Back when Jerry Seinfeld was a touring comic, he used a calendar system called "Don't break the chain." He marked each day on a calendar that he worked toward a goal. As you mark the days, you will not only track your progress but also appreciate the daily work you have put into your aspirations. After a while you'll have a long "chain" of days where you've completed a specific task or taken another step toward your goals. The aim here is to not "break the chain" by not missing days along the way.

8. **Kick-start the morning with exercise.** Exercising in the morning can be a quick way to get your blood moving and your brain awake and ready for action. You don't have to go to the gym for a full-on early morning workout, but even something as simple as a fifteen-minute run around your neighborhood or a brief cardio routine at home is enough to get your heart rate up and let your body know that it's time to be up and moving.

TIPS FOR EARLIER MORNINGS

Waking up earlier gives you more hours in the day and consequently more time to accomplish everything you want to. While you know that you should get out of bed at a decent time in the morning, actually doing so is easier said than done. Here are a few ways to make it happen:

9. Sleep with your curtains open. The natural sunlight will help gently wake you up in the morning.

10. If your bed isn't in direct view of a window (or you need to rise before the sun), use a dawn simulator to mimic the sun rising in your bedroom.

11. Going from waking up at eight a.m. to waking up at five a.m. is hard. Try gradually adjusting your wake-up time (fifteen minutes earlier each day, for example) until you reach your ideal.

12. Have a schedule of things you want to do once you get up. If you have specific tasks that need to be accomplished, you'll be less likely to snooze and miss them.

13. Stay off your phone before bed. Going immediately from your phone to bed will prevent you from falling asleep, which means you won't get all that precious beauty sleep you need.

14. Avoid alcohol before bed, as it can disrupt your sleep and make it harder to get up in the morning.

15. Have a definitive reason why you plan to get up earlier. Will it make you healthier? Give you more time with your kids? When you know the reason for doing something, it can be a powerful motivator in actually doing it.

16. Limit your caffeine intake after lunch so you're not still going strong late at night when you should be sleeping.

17. Adjust the thermostat in your bedroom to get warmer (during warm months) or colder (during cold months) when it's time for you to wake up. The change in temperature will make you want to get up and move elsewhere.

18. Set two alarms: one to wake you up and one to get you out of bed. Use the time between the two to reflect and mentally prepare for the day ahead.

19. **Create six "big picture" goals for the day.**
These can include both professional and personal goals. For instance, one of your goals might be to finish a big work project, while another might be to start planning your upcoming family vacation. The idea here is for you to give yourself a "big picture" vision of what you hope to accomplish so you can better steer your daily schedule and yourself toward those goals.

20. **Break your to-do list down into small, actionable steps.** For instance, instead of putting something like "work on the Rogers project" on your to-do list, break the task down into smaller, more specific steps like "email the Rogers client," "schedule a call with Smith about the Rogers project," and "research stats for the Rogers project." By breaking down the larger item, you're thinking through the details of what needs to get done. You'll also feel a lot more accomplished when you've knocked off ten items from your to-do list before lunch rather than none because you're still working on that same large task.

21. **Set ninety-day goals rather than yearly ones.**
Everything can change in a year. While many
of us spend the beginning of the year creating goals for what we hope to accomplish
by December 31, it's better to set goals you'd
like to finish by March 31 instead. Come April,
you can evaluate how close you are to reach-
ing those goals (if you haven't reached them
already) and revamp them—or create new
goals—for continued success in the following
three months. Even if you haven't reached your
original goal, you're now on track to reach it in
the next time frame.

22. **Remembering passwords can be difficult, especially if you have a number of different ones
to keep track of.** A password manager, such as
the app 1Password, can not only keep track of
your passwords but also help you come up with
supersecure passwords. There's nothing worse
than needing access to a tool and having to
waste time searching for the password or resetting it so you can get in.

23. **Eat right.** You've probably heard the saying "You get out of something what you put into it." That goes for your body as well. One of the cornerstones of being your most productive self is eating well. While grabbing a burger or takeout might be your fastest option, you're much better off ensuring that you eat healthy, nutritious meals that give your body and your mind the right kind of fuel to get things done throughout the day. After all, you are what you eat!

24. **Give each day a theme.** When each day has its own theme, it's easier to create your schedule for the week, stay on task, and make sure none of the aspects of your job are overshadowed by another. For instance, Mondays might be for looking for new business, while Tuesdays might be for meeting with your staff and/or clients or reviewing the business you already have. Using themes can also help you stay in the right headspace throughout the day since you won't be switching gears constantly.

25. **Leave your car keys with important materials you need to bring with you.** You can't be productive when you've left crucial items behind. Keeping your keys with those items ensures that when you're on the hunt for the keys in the morning, you'll be reminded to bring those important things with you when you head off to work.

✔ ✔ ✔

26. **Set all of your recurring bills up on autopay.** If a service you use doesn't offer an autopay option but you always pay the same amount, you can set up your own version of autopay using your bank's Bill Pay feature. When you don't have to spend time paying bills every month, you have more time to focus on other tasks.

27. **Save longer online articles for your downtime.**
Thanks to modern technology, information
from a variety of different news organizations
is always at your fingertips. It's great to read
those longer articles on current events and
cultural perspectives, but it can also take a ton
of time. Use the downtime, whether it is while
you're on the elliptical at the gym or on the
train commuting home, to enjoy those saved
articles (or blog posts or videos). You're saving
yourself time in a moment when you need to
be productive while giving yourself something
entertaining to do later on.

✓ ✓ ✓

28. **Be honest.** Lying might seem like a solution in
the moment, but it will come back to get you
later. If you tell your boss a project is almost
done when you haven't started, he will think
you're ready to take on more work. Honesty will
save you time and potential awkwardness or a
loss of credibility when you have to dig yourself
out from under the lie later.

29. **Track your accomplishments.** Inevitably during the day you're going to accomplish a lot of tasks that aren't on your to-do list but still need to be done. Whenever you do anything productive (no matter how small), write it down. By the end of the day, you'll have a long list of accomplishments to celebrate, even if some of them weren't things you originally set out to do. Those reminders of your productivity can be a motivating boost in keeping up your good work!

☑ ☑ ☑

30. **Schedule your errands based on location.** For instance, if you have to drop your son off at soccer practice in a town where your optometrist also happens to be, then perhaps you can pick up your contact prescription while he's practicing rather than the day before or after. If the grocery store is next door to where your daughter takes piano lessons, then you should make a habit of grocery shopping while she is at a lesson. Planning tasks around a location can cut down on your commute and overall time spent on a task.

31. **Let your calendar do the remembering.** No one can remember everything. Whenever a new task comes up, add time to work on that task to your calendar. For tasks that can't be specifically scheduled, set a reminder for yourself for a time or date when you aim to accomplish that task by. For instance, if you want to call a restaurant tomorrow to make a reservation, set a reminder for late in the afternoon to do it, just in case you lose track of time or forget about it.

32. **Give everything a dedicated place in your home or office.** You don't necessarily have to have a place for every single item, but try to at least organize things by general location. For instance, keep all of your power cables in a specific drawer in your desk, or all of the manuals you own in a specific box in your bedroom closet. When you need a new charging cable for your phone or instructions for the air conditioner, you'll at least have a general idea of where to look to find it a lot faster.

33. **Create a shared grocery list with your family.** Ideally, this is a digital list that everyone can access on the phone or computer. Since everyone can add to it, when one person finds herself at the store (or with the time to go to the store), she can grab everything the family needs so multiple trips aren't necessary. There are a number of different apps out there that allow you to make shared lists, including Evernote and Google Keep.

34. **Keep your "enemies" closer.** You can often learn a lot from your competition. Make a point to surround yourself with people who have viewpoints different from your own. If you have a colleague in a similar position whom you always butt heads with, try to work on teams with him rather than avoiding him. When you can see someone else's perspective on an issue, you'll be much better at finding an equitable solution for everyone involved. Hearing outside perspectives and learning from them can also sharpen your own perspective on a particular issue. When your solution takes multiple viewpoints into account from the beginning, it's less likely to need revising later down the line.

35. **Make sure your daily to-do list includes a step toward a larger goal.** This way you're doing something small in the moment, but you're also setting the stage to complete a much larger project in the future. For instance, if you have the larger goal of being fluent in German before your business trip to Berlin in five months, then block off time each day to work on it. Not all goals can be attained overnight!

36. **Hold regular check-in meetings with your family to discuss family business.** Set biweekly or monthly meetings with everyone to talk about upcoming family events and whatever else is on their minds. This can be as simple as making sure everyone has a ride home from school for the week or as involved as planning your next family vacation. When your family members are all on the same page, you save everyone the time and stress of haphazardly trying to deal with issues in the moment.

37. **If you have a drink you really enjoy after work, consider mixing up several at the beginning of the week and keeping them in the fridge so they're ready to go when you get home.** This obviously won't work for everything, but drinks like margaritas or even Negronis can be mixed together in larger batches and stored in your fridge. Premade cocktails are also great when you have last-minute guests and will allow you to focus on your friends, not your bartending skills (or lack thereof). Who knew margaritas could actually be productive?

✔ ✔ ✔

38. **Set items you use regularly to autoship to your home when you know you'll be almost out.** Many retailers now offer subscriptions to a number of household items like toilet paper, razors, and dish soap. If you don't want to commit to having something autoshipped, Amazon's Dash Buttons are a great alternative. Keep the Buttons in places like your laundry room for detergent and your bathroom for toilet paper; your family members can tap the Button when they notice the supply is running low, and Amazon will send a replacement before it runs out.

TIPS FOR STAYING ORGANIZED

When you can't find something you need or aren't sure where to begin and what to prioritize, you can't possibly be productive. Keeping even a little bit of organization in your life will go a long way toward your success. Here are some easy ways to stay organized:

39. Don't let things pile up. If you're putting off tasks, find a way to either tackle them ASAP or pass them along to someone else who can.

40. File paperwork as soon as you can. The more you let things accumulate on your desk, the harder it will be to get organized (or find certain papers) later on.

41. Keep a donation box tucked away in a closet at home where you and other family members can drop things that you know you no longer need.

42. Clean out your fridge weekly to make sure you don't have expired food hanging around. You don't want to plan on a breakfast with that bottle of OJ, only to discover it expired last month!

43. Before your kids go to bed at night, hold a "race" to see who can pick up and put away the most out-of-place stuff (e.g., toys and stray shoes) the fastest.

44. Organize your closet by occasion rather than item. When all your formal wear is together, it will be easier to find something for that big night out.

45. If something is broken and you don't have immediate plans to fix it, get rid of it. Don't keep things because you might repair them "one day."

46. If you have a lot to organize, start small, like organizing one desk drawer at a time. By the end of the week you will have an organized desk and will be ready to tackle that bookshelf.

47. Store things you use ten times a year or less in long-term storage like a garage or remote closet. Don't give those items prime real estate in your home!

48. Use hanging shoe organizers that go over the back of doors to organize office supplies, cables, and more.

49. **Think through what you want to say in emails before you type them out.** Far too often we quickly respond to messages thinking we're being more efficient, but the speed of our response means that we forget things in the note or aren't as clear as we can be. When you think through that message before sending it, you're making sure that your point gets across in email number one and you don't get sucked into a longer email chain where you have to clarify your original point.

50. **Make key people like your spouse, parent, or child "favorites" in your phone.** When you do, you can put your phone in Do Not Disturb mode whenever you need to without the fear that you'll accidentally miss an urgent call or text from that person. Do Not Disturb mode can be an exceptionally useful feature in ensuring that your phone doesn't constantly grab your attention during the day and disrupt what you're working on. Those important calls and texts from favorites will still get through, but all the unimportant noise will be filtered out.

51.

Create an evening routine for what you do right before bed. Routines aren't just for your work-day. An evening routine can help put your body in the mindset for bed so you fall asleep much fast-er. For instance, you might take the dog out for a quick stroll at eight thirty p.m., then have a cup of tea at nine p.m. and read a chapter of a book to wind down. The more you stick to your rou-tine, the more you'll get used to it and the easier it will become.

5 2 .   **Give yourself plenty of access to natural light during the day.** Humans aren't built to spend the day closed up in dark, windowless offices. Make it a point to get outside during the day to take in some sunlight. While you might not have that corner office, try to sit near windows whenever possible to experience sunlight during the workday. Exposure to the sun regulates your vitamin D levels, improving your mood, reducing stress, and helping you focus more. It is also essential to maintaining healthy bones.

5 3 .   **Carry a small pad of paper and a pen with you at all times.** This way you can jot down notes and to-dos while you're out and about so they're not forgotten. You can also create a digital version on your phone using your phone's Notes app or another note-taking app such as Google Keep.

54. **Don't be a multitasker.** A study by Stanford researchers found that people who multitasked were more distracted and had a harder time remembering what they were doing than those who didn't multitask. Instead of doing two or more things simultaneously, do one task and then move on to the next. By giving each task your complete focus, you'll do a better job *and* get everything done faster.

55. **Learn your grocery store.** If you always shop at the same place, learn where things are located in the store and then create your shopping list based on those locations. So, if your grocery has eight aisles, then your grocery list will have eight sections. By organizing your list based on where an item is in the store, you can make one quick and efficient trip rather than constantly running back to get that "one thing" on your list you overlooked a few aisles back.

5 6. **Take a cold shower.** Yes, hot showers are far more enjoyable; however, cold showers are known to increase your alertness and improve your immune system and circulation while also easing stress. If you find yourself in need of a focus or energy boost, try taking a five- to ten-minute cold shower to get your blood flowing. When you're done, you'll feel refreshed and ready to tackle the rest of your day.

5 7. **Follow the two-minute rule.** In general, if tasks come along that can be done in two minutes or less, you should do them immediately. The act of adding an item to your to-do list and coming back to it later will take up the better part of two minutes anyway. Completing tasks immediately will keep your to-do list short and your day moving along.

5 8 .   **Learn how to speed-read.** Being able to process large amounts of text in short periods of time can dramatically increase your productivity and give you more time to focus on other tasks. There are tons of books and tools out there to help you learn the skill. One easy way to get started is to put a white index card above the line you're currently reading. The card will block out what you've already read and keep your eyes moving down the page.

✓   ✓   ✓

5 9 .   **Chew gum.** Gum can increase the amount of oxygen that is sent to your brain, giving you an extra boost of energy so you can better focus on the task at hand.

60. **Sit next to someone who is being productive.** That person's productivity isn't going to physically rub off on you, but sitting next to someone who is head-down on a project and working hard will inspire you to do the same. No one wants to be the guy browsing *Facebook* next to someone who is pumping out a hundred-page report. Productivity is contagious—just find somewhere to sit where you can catch it!

61. **Enlist a money manager.** Money is one of the biggest points of stress in life. Hiring a money manager to help you handle your finances can be a great way to set yourself up for success down the line. She can help you reach your savings and investment goals and make smart decisions about your future.

6 2 .   **Get up to (typing) speed.** Being a slow typer will impede almost everything you do in a work setting as well as sometimes in your personal life. You'll be slower at responding to chat messages, slower at responding to emails, and slower at writing reports. Learning how to type faster is just a matter of teaching your hands where the different letters are on the keyboard. If you know you're slow, try to spend a few minutes each day practicing. There are a number of different online tools out there that can help you learn and sharpen your skills.

☑ ☑ ☑

6 3 .   **Make a timed playlist to use when completing certain tasks.** Instead of using a timer or clock to keep track of the time, use music to make things more enjoyable and to avoid continually looking at the clock while you work. For instance, you might have a ten-minute playlist for taking a shower in the morning or a thirty-minute playlist you listen to while you're preparing dinner. Over time your mind and body will learn that a certain song means that you need to get up and get dressed or that it's almost time to go to work.

6 4 .   **Practice a self-affirming exercise.** At the end of each day, ask yourself if you think you gave that day your best effort. If you did, then this is a great way to motivate yourself to be even more productive tomorrow. If you didn't, then you can pinpoint places where you had trouble during the day and focus on overcoming those obstacles tomorrow. When you constantly strive to do your best, it shows. Strive to have more and more days where you can say you did the best you could!

6 5 .   **Get feedback from others.** The only way to get better at something is to know where you need to improve, and it's often hard to highlight your own shortcomings. Instead, always seek out feedback from others, be they coworkers, family members, or people you're just serving on a committee with. Just asking the simple question "How could I be doing better here?" can give you insight into not only what you're excelling at but also what you can work on going forward.

66. **Take a personal day.** If your personal to-do list starts to get out of hand, consider taking a day off from work to tackle it. The whole point of taking a vacation is to cut down on stress. If your personal stress is starting to become too much to handle, then taking a vacation day to knock things off your to-do list can actually help you de-stress better than taking a day off to relax on the beach.

☑ ☑ ☑

67. **Take your time.** Working quickly doesn't always mean you're being your most productive. When you move too fast, you often miss things in the process and make mistakes. Slow down on important tasks so that you can really give them the attention they deserve. This way you ensure the job is done right (and well) the first time!

TIPS TO KEEP YOU MOTIVATED

Motivation is key to being your most productive self. When you are feeling motivated, you are able to push through distractions and other obstacles to complete a task. Here are a few easy ways to keep yourself motivated when you feel your attention waning:

68. If you start to get discouraged about something, list the reasons why you're doing that thing in the first place.

69. Consider why you were selected to do a job. What makes you the best fit for it? Show off those skills!

70. Has someone completed a similar task in the past? How did the person do it? Follow his example.

71. Take a virtual walk in someone else's shoes. If you're starting to feel burned out on a particular project, look at it from a different person's perspective (perhaps the person you're completing the task for). Remembering why your project matters can be just what you need to reach the finish line.

72. Walk away from the task for a few minutes and do something else. When you get a bit of space from something, you often come back with a renewed energy to complete it.

73. Look at the task with a "fresh" pair of eyes. Imagine that you're just starting the project and think about the best ways to tackle it. You just might see a solution that you didn't before.

74. Consider what rewards you'll get once you're finished. Envisioning the achievement of a job finished—and finished well—can be just what you need for an extra boost of productivity.

75. Picture yourself completing the project. How does it feel? Work toward that feeling!

76. Make your goal public. Knowing that other people are aware that you're working toward something can be a great motivator in pushing you to reach that goal.

77. Treat yourself to a little gift, like a latte at the coffee shop downstairs or a few minutes browsing *Instagram*, for finishing that task. When you're working toward something you want, you'll be motivated to keep at it.

78. **Scale back the time you spend on something to make it more manageable.** For instance, if you don't think you can fully focus on a certain task for one full hour, try working on it for twenty-minute intervals instead.

☑ ☑ ☑

79. **Get some sleep.** Sleep is one of the most important things you need to guarantee you have a productive day—don't cheat yourself out of it. If you don't get enough, you're going to be groggy, easily distracted, and not your best self in general. Make getting seven to eight hours of sleep every night a priority.

CHAPTER 2

STAYING PRODUCTIVE AT WORK

80. **Come in early.** If you can, try to arrive at the office before everyone else. Being one of the first people to arrive in the morning gives you the opportunity to enjoy the "calm" before the "storm." You can often get more work done before others in the office—and the distractions that they bring—arrive. Coming in early also gives you the opportunity to ease into your day rather than having to hit the ground running at full speed.

81. **Hide your phone during the workday.** When you get to the office, put your personal phone in a desk drawer or bag and try to leave it there, pulling it out only during lunch or other breaks. Even when you're not getting messages or calls, having your phone nearby can make it tempting to check social media or other websites while you should be working. If you can keep your phone on silent and out of sight, it will stay off your mind.

82. **Sign up for direct deposit.** Most banks will allow you to deposit checks via their mobile apps, but even that can be an unnecessary waste of time. If your office offers direct deposit, make sure you sign up. Besides direct deposit saving you the time of physically making the deposit on your own, in most cases people with direct deposit actually get paid a tiny bit faster than those who get paid via paper check.

83. **Don't be afraid to delegate.** When you're working on a project, it can be easy to think that you and you alone need to complete it. If there are portions of the project that can be completed by someone else, don't be afraid to ask another person to handle them. For instance, things like making copies or filing reports can be handled by an intern. This will allow you to focus your attention on the larger portions.

TIPS FOR GETTING PROMOTED

Promotions are great, but it's often hard to know just what to say and do to get that ball rolling. If you have been in your current position for a while and are itching to move up, there are a few proactive things you can do to fast-track that promotion:

84. Find someone in a position similar to the one you want and ask what she did to achieve it.

85. Dress for the position. No one wants to hire a manager who looks like an intern. Dress the part. If you look like someone in a higher position, people will start to think of you as being in that position.

86. Participate. If you're gunning for a promotion, then make sure you're participating in every project that comes your way and giving it your all.

87. Be personable. No one likes a brownnose, but a little kindness can go a long way. Make a point to be pleasant to all your coworkers and managers.

88. Be a helper. If a coworker is having trouble with a task you can handle, assist him. Your helpfulness won't go unnoticed.

89. If you highlight a problem at work, be prepared with a solution. You don't want to be known as the guy who brings the problems; you want to be the one who brings the solutions.

90. Be a team player. If there's an office happy hour or birthday celebration, make sure you're in attendance. One element of success in the workplace is being a part of the office "family."

91. Learn as much as you can about the position and the requirements. If it's in a field that requires a specific level of expertise, make sure your training exceeds that level.

92. Be prepared to go the extra mile. If your boss is looking for volunteers for an unpleasant task, make sure your name is at the top of the list.

93. Build others up; don't knock them down. Don't try to climb over others to get that promotion. Instead, support those around you. When you do, you'll be surprised by how those people are willing to help build you up too.

94. **Keep noise-canceling headphones or ear-buds in your desk.** Even the quietest offices can be distracting during the day. Not only will headphones help you drown everyone out, but having them on also sends a silent message to others that you'd rather not be disturbed unless it's absolutely necessary.

95. **Admit when you don't understand or know how to do something.** Claiming to understand a topic or process you don't can severely hurt your productivity simply because you now have to spend time learning a skill you said you already had. When you don't know, say so. The asker can either delegate the task to someone who is familiar with the process or help you learn what you need to get the job done.

96. **Take vacations! It seems a bit counterintuitive, but one of the greatest things you can do to maintain productivity is to take days off on a regular basis.** Working for months on end without a vacation can lead to burnout and apathy when it comes to your job and the tasks that come along with it. Be sure to take time off to completely disconnect from the office. When you do return, you'll be refreshed—possibly with new ideas and a new energy toward your work.

☑ ☑ ☑

97. **Curb the coffee.** Just because your office kitchen has a fresh pot of coffee available all day long doesn't mean that you should drink it all day long. Caffeine can be a great way to get you going in the morning, but if you consume too much of it, you can end up so hyperactive that you're scattered in your work or so over-caffeinated that you crash hard when the caffeine finally starts to wear off. Try to limit your coffee consumption to just a cup or two early in the day and then switch to water or decaf for the rest of the day.

98. **Use your calendar for everything, not just specific appointments or meetings.** If you use your calendar just for scheduling meetings, you can quickly run into a situation where you don't have time to accomplish other tasks. Use your calendar to block off time for projects, just as if you were scheduling a meeting, so you have a clearer grasp of when you have time for new tasks or meetings.

99. **Schedule specific times during the workday to go through your email inbox.** Instead of checking your email constantly during the day, you could spend the second hour of your day and an hour right after lunch to check up on and respond to messages. If you restrict your email use, you avoid getting sucked into responding to messages throughout the day.

100. **Snap a photo of any business cards you're given so you don't misplace them.** Business cards are easy to collect and hard to find when you need them. With a photo, you'll never lose a person's contact information. You can also create a virtual "contact" profile with this picture and information about where you met the person, links to the person's professional websites or online profiles, and more.

101. **Consider working from home for a few days.** Going to the office has obvious benefits, but sometimes you can get more work done by cutting out your commute and working from home instead. If you're working on a large project and having trouble completing it at the office, consider moving your "operation" to your home for a few days. The change of scenery can give you a new perspective and eliminates traditional office distractions like chatty coworkers.

WAYS TO REGAIN YOUR FOCUS

When you're working in an office, it's inevitable that at some point you're going to lose your focus. Whether it's a large project that's overwhelmed you to the point of confusion or frustration, or an annoying coworker who hit a nerve after his twentieth interruption of the day, setbacks happen. Here are a few ways to get your thinking back on track:

102. Take a minute to reassess your task. Write down what you've completed so far, and remind yourself of what needs to get done now.

103. Take a quick lap around your office building. The physical activity will help your brain reset. You can also walk up and down a few flights of stairs in your building if a lap outside isn't possible.

104. Drink a glass of water. It's amazing how a little H_2O can refresh your mind.

105. Concentrate on your breathing: take thirty deep inhales and exhales before continuing what you're working on.

106. Take a break to listen to a song you enjoy. The short break will be just what you need to reset.

107. Tidy up your desk. Starting again with a clean workspace can help you concentrate on the task at hand.

108. Pinpoint the easiest aspect of the project and do that first. Once you've tackled a small portion of a task, the rest won't feel as overwhelming.

109. Close your office door and make yourself "invisible" on work chats and other websites.

110. If you're being interrupted at your desk, try moving to a conference room for an hour. If you're running into the same issue there, work at home for the rest of the day.

111. Spend a few minutes playing a video game. You don't want to pull out Mario Kart at the office, but video games (in short doses) have been proven to improve concentration and focus. Try playing a few minutes of a matching game like Candy Crush Saga or Mahjong on your phone to get your brain back into focus mode.

112. **Filter those emails!** When you get a significant amount of email each day, it can be easy for important messages to get lost in the shuffle, putting you behind in your work. At a minimum, set up filters so emails from regular business contacts and colleagues go to their own priority inbox. When you have filters set up, you can be sure that you see the messages you need to in a timely manner.

113. **Just because something has "always" been done a certain way in your office doesn't mean that it's the right way.** If you see a way to streamline something that's already being done in your office and make it better, speak up. Too often we get stuck in the way things are done and don't think about how those ways can be improved.

114. **Restructure your job.** If there are parts of your job that you don't enjoy doing, chances are you're less efficient at them simply because they don't interest you. If you find there's a task that is a constant speed bump in your day, examine why you dislike doing it and see if there's a way to make it better. For instance, if you hate filling out spreadsheets, it might be because you don't really understand how to use Excel. Make time to learn some tips and tricks from a spreadsheet pro in your office. Afterward, you may not dread Excel as much, and you'll be able to complete spreadsheet tasks faster in the future.

✓ ✓ ✓

115. **Create canned email responses.** If you find yourself constantly responding to messages in a specific way, having a preset response lets you answer those emails more efficiently and can guarantee that you don't accidentally leave out key details. Many email programs allow you to save these canned responses for quick sending. If your program doesn't, write some up and save them in the Notes app on your computer for easy access.

116. **Stand up.** If you get stuck in a conversation with a colleague that's taking up too much of your time, an easy solution is to simply stand up. Standing up gives the other person the impression that you're about to head out to a meeting or some other engagement, and it will encourage the person to wrap up her thoughts and move along.

117. **When you meet a new business contact, send that person an email the next day.** In your note mention where you met him and what you talked about. Besides being a classy networking move, the email is a great way for that person to remember you. Plus, now that you've emailed the person, you can search your inbox later for the name of the event or the topic of conversation and find his email address even if you've forgotten his name (it happens).

118. **Just pick up the phone.** If there's an email that you're actively avoiding, or one that will take a lot of time to respond to, call the person instead. A phone conversation can be much faster than email and can eliminate the back-and-forth that often comes with digital communication. An email that might have taken you thirty minutes to write can likely be handled with a ten-minute phone call.

☑ ☑ ☑

119. **Whenever you create a new goal, make sure that it's a S.M.A.R.T. one.** S.M.A.R.T. goals were first mentioned in a paper by George T. Doran in *Management Review*. The idea is that you're creating the right goals by making sure each one fits within the acronym S.M.A.R.T., which stands for "specific, measurable, achievable, realistic, and time-bound." If a goal meets those criteria, then it's something worth working toward. Define S.M.A.R.T. goals with your manager to help improve your skills and grow your career.

120.

Carry a business card. Even if you aren't in a career position where you regularly need to pass out business cards, get some anyway and make sure you always have a handful in your wallet or purse. You never know when you might encounter someone who could be a business contact. Good connections can be made at a bar after work, at a high school friend's wedding, or even while you're out to dinner with your family. Having a card on hand means you won't miss an opportunity.

121. **Find a mentor.** It's easy to get stagnant in a position, losing the motivation or know-how to move yourself to the next level. Find someone a few steps above you on your desired career path and ask that person to be a mentor. A mentor can help make suggestions on what you should do next so you're not wasting time doing things that don't get you to your ultimate goal.

122. **Try the Pomodoro Technique for long-term projects.** Francesco Cirillo's Pomodoro Technique has long been a favorite of productivity enthusiasts. The idea behind it is that the easiest way to stay productive when working on a task is to work on it in blocks of time rather than all at once. Specifically, it suggests that you work for twenty-five minutes, then give yourself a five-minute break. Incorporating regular breaks will allow you to refresh and tackle each work "session" with a rejuvenated mind.

123. **Meditate.** You don't need to do a full-on thirty-minute or hour-long meditation to get the benefits. If things in the office start to get overwhelming, spending just a few minutes listening to soothing sounds or music and focusing on your thoughts can help you then stay focused on your work for the remainder of the day. There are a ton of apps that guide you through short meditations, or you can create your own meditation by closing your office door, listening to soothing music with your headphones on, and concentrating on your breathing for a few minutes.

124. **When a project gets overwhelming, walk away.** If you're working on a larger project and find yourself spinning your wheels, sometimes it's better to just walk away from it for the rest of the day and try again in the morning. Stopping work may seem counterintuitive, but taking a long break to work on something else or assist a coworker can help you come back with a new perspective so you can move forward with the project.

125. **Be the "power user" for all of the software tools your office uses.** If you don't take the time to learn how to use a new tool, then you're likely to waste more time trying to figure it out down the line than you would have if you just did some training earlier. Plus, when you don't learn a new tool and everyone else does, you'll find yourself trying to catch up when others are able to accomplish the same work faster.

126. **Learn from your colleagues.** Is someone you work with getting similar tasks done much faster? Ask the person how she does it. Even if you don't adopt the method, learning how someone else is accomplishing a similar task can act as inspiration for you in coming up with a new way to work that's all your own!

127. **Take a walk.** Even a short walk around your office building can give you enough space from a project to come back with a fresh perspective. A walk can also help break up the monotony of sitting at your desk all day and convince your brain that you're starting something new, rather than continuing to plug away at the same problem that's plagued your entire morning.

128. **Eat a light lunch.** While it can be tempting to get that steak on the company dime at a lunch meeting, try to stick to something lighter whenever possible. A big meal around lunch might taste delicious, but it leads to lethargy once you make it back to the office afterward. Light lunch fare like salads and soup will fill you up without weighing you down and set you up for a productive afternoon.

129. **Block time-sucking websites on your work computer.** It can be hard to stay totally off social media during work, but do your best to block or limit your office access to websites like *Facebook* and *Twitter*. If you find it's impossible not to check them during the day, start by limiting your use to your breaks.

130. **Set a specific time frame to work on a project.** When that time frame is over, move on to the next task, even if you haven't completed that first task. For instance, if you're working on a report and have allocated one hour for the job, once that hour is over, move on to the next item on your to-do list. This will give you insight into which tasks are slowing you down so you can either make time adjustments or figure out if there is a larger issue behind why they are taking you longer than anticipated.

131. **Set fake deadlines.** For instance, if a big project is due on Friday morning, tell yourself (and any subordinates) that it needs to be completed by Wednesday afternoon instead. Setting the earlier deadline gives you a little bit of a buffer if things do take longer than anticipated, and it gives you extra time to go over everything and guarantee that you're turning in the best work possible rather than what you were able to squeeze out by the deadline.

☑ ☑ ☑

132. **Plan for your problems.** If you're working on a long-term project that will likely need a few able folks to complete, set up a "flight crew" for it just as if the project were a plane (every plane crew member has a designated job in case of an emergency). Once you know who is in your crew, set up regular, short meetings with them. This way you can keep them up to date on the details of the project and give them a heads-up if their help is going to be needed soon (which saves you from having to chase people down when you need them).

133. Pick the best person for the job. If you're in charge of assigning work projects, assign tasks based on who you think would do the best job rather than job title and seniority. The office "people person," for instance, might be best at making client calls, while a detail-focused colleague might be better at looking through a big report and spotting errors. When you consider employee personalities when assigning tasks, they're likely to be much happier with their tasks and will do them much more efficiently.

134. Defuse drama! Office drama not only causes problems in the moment but can also make working with that individual much less efficient going forward. If you have a disagreement with a coworker, address it with her as soon as possible and involve a mediator if need be. Be polite and respectful, and try to understand the other person's point of view. In the end, you're looking for a solution that improves your working relationship with that person—you don't have to be friends, but you do need to be able to work together well.

135. **Start large projects at the beginning of the week.** When you start a big project in the middle or at the end of the week, you're adding to others' to-do lists (as well as your own) late in the game. Individuals you need focus from are likely committed elsewhere, and everyone is starting to wind down for the weekend. When you start projects early in the week, people are refreshed and have a full week to handle a new task instead of working on it for a few days and then losing momentum over the weekend. Get on others' to-do lists as soon as possible!

✓ ✓ ✓

136. **Schedule a "power hour."** If you're having trouble finding the time in your day to handle a collection of smaller projects, schedule an hour to hunker down and knock out all of those tasks that you can't quite find time for otherwise. The hour should go on your calendar just like any other important meeting—you mean business!

137. **Go all-in on company-specific tools.** If your company uses any specific tool for communication or organization, use it as much as possible. For instance, if your company uses Slack for interoffice communication, communicate with your colleagues exclusively through that tool rather than through email or another instant messaging service. This way you have only one program to pay attention to for messages and conversations. The fewer services you have to keep track of, the easier it will be to monitor them.

☑ ☑ ☑

138. **Check in with yourself midweek.** The goals that we set for ourselves on Monday may have completely changed by Wednesday. Set aside fifteen minutes on Wednesday to look at what your goals were for the week on Monday and where you are in your quest to achieve them. If you've fallen behind, look at responsibilities you can possibly pass off to a coworker or assistant to get you back on track. If you're ahead of schedule, think about how you're going to fill that extra time later in the week.

139. **Take advantage of your lunch hour.** Use a lunch meeting to chat with your mentor or meet with your chattier coworkers so that they'll be less inclined to bother you during the rest of the day. This frees up time in the afternoon!

☑ ☑ ☑

140. **Assign tasks to that office chatterbox.** If you have a coworker who keeps interrupting you while you're working, suggest a task for him to help you with. Clearly if someone keeps interrupting your workflow, then he has some additional time on his hands. You'll have one thing taken off your plate, and knowing that a visit to your office is likely to result in busywork will also make the person think twice about interrupting you again in the future.

141. **Bookmark frequently used online tools.** A
good rule of thumb is to make the sites you visit
daily part of the bookmarks bar on your browser while saving the ones you need only once
a week or less as traditional bookmarks. Most
browsers will also let you "pin" a tab—this keeps
a site "permanently" open on your browser so
you won't accidentally close it.

142. **Get rid of screen distractions.** If you find yourself getting distracted by other things on your
computer screen, go "full screen" with the program you're using. When the program takes up
the entire screen, you won't get distracted by
your growing inbox or other notifications while
you're trying to work.

THINGS PRODUCTIVE PEOPLE HAVE ON THEIR DESK

Productivity starts with your work area. Here are a few useful items to keep on your desk to boost your efficiency:

143. A second monitor. An extra monitor allows you to have multiple browser windows and apps open at once so you don't have to weed through twenty tabs to find something.

144. Sticky notes. These are great for writing yourself small reminders or project notes that you attach to your monitor or project folder.

145. A pack of highlighters in various colors. Countless studies have shown the link between color and memory. Assigning different projects to colors on your calendar or in your personal notes can help you keep track of all the different tasks and things to remember throughout your day.

146. A portable stand to turn your sitting desk into a standing desk. Research has found that switching from sitting to standing throughout the day can boost energy levels as well as mood.

147. Cables to charge all your electronic gadgets.

148. A calming figurine, Zen garden, or plant that you can focus on when you need a brief refresher between tasks.

149. A backup hard drive where your work is routinely saved. This way, if your computer experiences technical difficulties, you'll still have access to your work.

150. A lamp. Even if you have a wall full of windows, a lamp will come in handy when you're working late. Turning it on while reading paper documents can also provide an extra boost of alertness when your mind starts to wander.

151. A filing system. For instance, you might have a basket for incoming mail and another for correspondence you need to deal with. Don't ever let papers just aimlessly sit on your desk while you're not using them. That's how things get lost and how you end up wasting valuable time finding them.

152. A few snacks. You don't want to keep twelve bags of chips in your desk drawer, but a few protein bars or packages of peanuts will come in handy when you start to get hungry but don't have time to step away from your desk to find a snack.

153. **Show your appreciation.** If you manage employees, one of the best things you can do to increase productivity is to be sure they know you appreciate their hard work. Appreciation can be anything from verbally acknowledging the great job they did to taking them out to lunch to celebrate a job well done. Employees who feel valued in their positions are happier at work and work hard to do their best for you.

154. **Move your space.** If you find that you're seated next to a chatterbox who's making it hard for you to get work done, ask your boss about moving your workspace. Everyone wants you to be your most productive self while you're at work, and your boss will likely be happy to help you find a better spot where you can focus. If another chair isn't in the regular office space, consider relocating for a few hours to an available conference room or another quiet spot in your office.

155.

Put your computer on Do Not Disturb mode. Just like your phone, your computer has a handy Do Not Disturb mode. Activate it when you really need to focus on a project so that you aren't distracted by constant notifications.

CHAPTER 3

BEING PRODUCTIVE WHEN YOU WORK FROM HOME

156. **Enforce a work "schedule" at home.** Just because you're working from home doesn't mean that you shouldn't have a work schedule. If you're working for a traditional employer, then chances are you have set hours you need to work each day. If you're not working for a traditional employer, set hours that work for the type of business you're in. Having a regular routine will motivate you to get started at an appropriate hour and work a normal "shift" just like you would at a traditional office.

157. **Communicate your schedule to your family.** Once you've established your work schedule, make sure everyone in your household knows that those are your work hours and you're not to be disturbed during that time. When everyone at home knows your work hours, they're much more likely to respect them. Additionally, having a schedule established with your family will hold you more accountable for sticking to those hours.

158. **Get dressed up.** When people think of working from home, they often think of curling up with a laptop in bed and spending their day in comfy pajamas. Don't do this! You don't need to put on a three-piece suit to work from your home office, but you should shower and change into regular clothes. Getting dressed will put you in the right mindset for getting work done, helping you make the transition from "home time" to "work time."

✓ ✓ ✓

159. **Try commuting to your home office.** Help get yourself in the mood for work by creating a commute to your home office. The commute can be something as simple as leaving the house for a walk around the block or heading down the street to grab a cup of coffee. The simple act of leaving your house for a few minutes can help your mind move from "relax mode" to "business mode" and will make you much more focused when you sit down to begin work.

160. **Close the door!** If you have your own home office, the best way to deal with everything from those dishes that need to be washed to a spouse or kids who want your attention is to simply close the door. A closed door will help send the message to other members of your household that you're busy and shouldn't be disturbed; it also will help you focus by creating a workspace somewhat separated from all the home and family distractions outside.

161. **Keep friends away during your workday.** When making plans with friends, agree only to plans that you might have made if you were working in a traditional office. For instance, if you plan to meet a friend for lunch, go to a restaurant rather than having that friend over. While an at-home lunch is convenient, your friend will naturally feel like he can stay longer than a traditional lunch hour. The same goes for having friends stop by during the day. If your friend wouldn't have stopped by your office downtown, then he shouldn't drop by your home during your workday either.

162.

Work during your hours of peak productivity. Some people are morning people, while others find they're significantly more productive at night. Working from home often means you have more wiggle room to figure out when you are most productive and adjust your schedule so that you're working (especially on your bigger projects) during those hours of peak productivity. You can then spend your less productive hours on simple tasks like responding to emails.

163. **Plan out everything.** When you work from home, you are your own secretary, so plan out things like email time and breaks so they feel more set in stone and you don't accidentally overcommit yourself. The more prepared your schedule is, the easier it will be to keep yourself on task!

164. **Look at the week from an environment perspective.** For instance, if your kids are off from school on Wednesday, then that's probably not the best day for you to plan to be in a number of video conferences. If you need to read a large report, that might be best saved for the five-hour cross-country flight you're taking on Tuesday afternoon. Making plans based on what will be happening around you helps you make the best use of your time and keeps things running much more smoothly.

165. **Make your office off-limits.** Having your children read books in the corner while you're plugging away at a project might not seem like a big deal, but their presence will be at the back of your mind, distracting you even if you aren't aware of it. Don't allow others to be in the same room with you while you're trying to get work done, even if they promise to be *extra* quiet. If you wouldn't have your husband read the newspaper across from your desk at the office, then he shouldn't be sitting across from your desk at home either.

☑ ☑ ☑

166. **Work near a window.** Keep in mind that while you want light, you don't want a distraction, so if there are a few windows to choose from, go with the most distraction-free option. Avoid windows that face a busy street or the bustling backyard of a next-door neighbor.

167. **Make your office yours.** If your home office is in your kid's outgrown bedroom or playroom, you're going to notice and be distracted by the decor. When you select a place for your dedicated home office, make it yours by painting the walls and decorating it in a way that supports your workflow. Create a space where you feel comfortable with as few distractions as possible. That means keeping your guitar and your video game system somewhere else.

✓ ✓ ✓

168. **Find an accountability buddy.** When you're working in an office, there's likely to be a number of people around who will notice if you've been watching online videos when you should be finishing a report. When you're at home, it's easier to fall into those traps simply because there's no one around to notice. Find a friend who works from home to cowork with you for the day. Websites like *Focusmate* and *GetMotivatedBuddies* can also pair you with someone virtually. You can sign up for web chats with someone who also works from home, explain what you're working on to each other, and then hold each other accountable for getting those tasks done.

TASKS TO DELEGATE TO AN ASSISTANT

If you find yourself constantly getting preoccupied by small tasks, consider hiring an assistant to tackle them for you so you can focus on more important work. Depending on the tasks you need help with, a personal assistant can be anyone from a high school or college student who helps you out for a few hours a week after school to a trained professional who works as a full-time assistant. Virtual assistants (people who can handle work for you from a remote location) are also a great option. Here are a few things you can ask an assistant to handle:

169. Booking flights

170. Researching hotels

171. Making copies

172. Running errands

173. Setting up meetings

174. Transcribing meeting and interview notes

175. Doing basic research for a project

176. Proofreading documents and reports

177. Shopping for office supplies

178. Responding to business inquiries

179. **Set up a weekly cleaning schedule for your home office.** Even the messiest people (no judgment!) can see a dirty window or an un-vacuumed floor as a good reason to procrastinate from the task at hand. Avoid giving yourself an unnecessary distraction by setting aside at least thirty minutes for the job. Do things that a cleaning service might do at a traditional office such as sweeping the floor, wiping the coffee rings off your desk, and emptying the garbage.

☑ ☑ ☑

180. **Hire a babysitter.** Even parents who work from home need babysitters! Just because you work from home doesn't always mean you're free to take care of your kids during work hours. If you have young children at home all day, hire someone who can watch them for at least a few hours a day or a few days a week. Having child-free time that you can truly dedicate to working is important for your focus and productivity.

181. **Schedule must-do tasks first.** When you know you're going to get that "one thing" done, then everything else will fall into place more easily. That "one thing" can also be something for yourself rather than work. If you really want to find time to get a haircut this week, start by scheduling the haircut and then organizing all your other tasks around it. The day you have that haircut, you're likely to be much more productive before you go simply because you know you need to step away from work by a certain time.

✓ ✓ ✓

182. **Invest in your home Internet.** A slow Internet plan often ends up being even slower than advertised during peak times and can really bog down your workflow. Buy the fastest Internet package you can reasonably afford. Since you're using it for work, part of that plan is tax deductible (or might even be covered by your employer). Fast Internet access is key when you want to have video conferences, have web chats, or upload or download huge files.

183. **Get a work-only phone line.** When you work from home, your home phone can quickly turn into your work phone. Having business calls come to your personal cell phone might not seem like a problem at first, but it means that you won't be able to turn them off when you're on vacation, and that you have to keep your personal cell by your side during work hours— which will be a distraction. Instead, consider getting a dedicated work number that you pass out to business-related contacts.

☑ ☑ ☑

184. **Buy a printer.** Yes, most things are done digitally these days, but that doesn't mean you shouldn't own a printer. You'd be surprised at how many times you find that you need to print something. Going to a copy shop to print just a few pages is a time-consuming and annoying process, even more so when you realize that the original printing has a small typo or needs to be changed. A decent printer isn't a huge expense and will be a big bonus when you need it.

185. **Splurge on a nice office chair.** Sitting for a prolonged period of time in a chair without proper support can cause you pain and even serious back issues down the line. Do yourself a favor and invest in an office chair that you're comfortable sitting in—you won't have to take as many breaks, and you will be much more productive than if you spent the day readjusting and thinking about how uncomfortable you are.

186. **Have a backup Internet plan in place.** No matter what company you use for Internet access, there will come a day when that access goes out for a few hours (or even days) for reasons out of your control. Having a cellular data plan that allows you to tether your computer to your mobile phone for Internet access is a great tool that traveling employees often use. It can make sure you're not unexpectedly MIA from the office in situations when you have critical meetings or deadlines.

187. **Use a dedicated browser for your work activities.** For instance, you might use Google Chrome exclusively for work and Safari exclusively for personal activities. Having a dedicated browser enables you to install browser plugins for a specific use and create a work-specific bookmarks bar that doesn't get in your way when you're surfing the web after work. It also allows you to block sites that distract you during work, but you still have access to them via your personal browser.

188. **Update your (work) status.** Most work-focused chat apps let you set a status message for your coworkers to see. Take advantage of this feature to let others know when you're "out to lunch" or "on a call" so that they know when they can expect a response from you. When people know that you maintain a current status on those messaging services, they'll be less likely to bug you when you've noted that you're unavailable.

189. **Try a standing desk.** Sitting all day can some-times get a bit too comfortable, ultimately making you less productive. Change things up during the day with a standing desk. Not only is standing while you're working healthier, but it can also help give you a boost of energy and get your creative juices flowing for a larger project. You don't have to purchase a dedicated standing desk—a tall countertop or shelf will do in a pinch.

190. **Turn your phone's ringer off when your work-day begins.** When your phone rings, your natu-ral inclination is to answer it. When you do, even if it's just for a quick call, you throw off your fo-cus from the task you were working on. Instead, silence your phone and have all your calls go to voice mail. Schedule a few times each day to look at your missed calls, listen to voice mail, and return those calls that need your attention.

191. **Schedule evening email responses to be sent the following morning.** When you work from home, sometimes the evening hours are the easiest to deal with email, but messages that are sent at night can be buried by a windfall of emails in the morning; schedule your email to be sent first thing in the morning so your recipient actually sees your message and it doesn't get lost in her inbox.

192. **Stock office snacks and drinks for the day.** Don't put yourself in a position where you're going to have to leave home during the day if you get hungry or need something to drink. At the beginning of the week make sure you have enough coffee and office snacks available for you to make it until Friday. You'll thank yourself come Thursday afternoon when you need to focus on a big project but also need coffee or a quick snack to make it happen.

193. **Use music to help you stay focused during the day.** Background noise can be exceptionally useful in drowning out sounds like a neighbor mowing his lawn or the kids fighting over the TV. Instead of the radio, opt for sounds and tunes without words. Classical music is a great choice, as is white noise like the sounds of ocean waves or a babbling brook. Find playlists online for distraction-free music to listen to throughout your day.

✓ ✓ ✓

194. **Cowork with others in a remote space.** Your home office can get monotonous, especially since you don't have coworkers to chat with during the day. The monotony can even lead to you becoming more easily distracted and significantly less productive. Switch things up every now and then by coworking with others in a place other than home. Coworking spaces are the perfect blend of working from home and working in an office. While you're still independently working, a coworking space can give you the accountability of having others around as well as access to tools like a printer and conference room.

195.

Pretend you're not home. Sometimes the easiest way to avoid distractions is to simply act like you're not at home. That means not answering the phone or the door during your working hours. Yes, you might miss a few things, but truth be told you would have missed the same things had you been working at a traditional office, and there's a good chance that what you miss (telemarketers and sales calls) isn't that important in the first place.

196. Don't let tiny problems become huge annoy-
ances. If something is irritating you in your
home like a leaky faucet, get it fixed immediately (not during your work hours, though!). When
there's a small annoyance around you, you're
likely to focus on it and get distracted from your
work until the problem is corrected. Save yourself some time, and fix problems (or schedule a
fix when you can!) as soon as possible.

197. Purchase a headset with a built-in micro-
phone to use for work-related conversations.
When you work from home, you'll find a number
of ambient sounds going on around you—things
like dogs barking and your neighbor repairing
his fence. While those sounds might not bother
you, they can make you seem unprofessional
on the phone. Do yourself and your business
contacts a favor and buy a headset to cut out
the background noise. You'll sound like you're
working from a "real" office, and you won't
have to spend time repeating things and explaining what all those weird sounds are.

MAKE-AHEAD LUNCHES FOR A FOCUSED DAY

Making your lunch ahead of time will take the stress out of lunchtime and ensure you have something delicious and nutritious to fuel the rest of your workday. Here are a few ideas for meals you can premake during the weekend and enjoy during the workweek:

198. A multiserving salad. Use healthy greens and vegetables to make a salad that will last for multiple lunches. If you want to add some protein into the mix, heat up some precooked chicken breast or other protein-packed leftovers to toss in right before you eat for a quick, warm meal.

199. Sandwich wraps. Wraps are easy to make and refrigerate ahead of time, and are a nice change from your average sandwich.

200. A pot of soup or chili. Make a huge portion of your favorite recipe during the weekend and divide it up into storage containers that can be quickly reheated at lunchtime.

201. Savory muffins. Muffins aren't just for breakfast. A muffin filled with cheese and ham is a delicious lunchtime treat that's easy to make and refrigerate.

202. Macaroni and cheese. Love mac and cheese? (Who doesn't?) Make a family-sized pan during the weekend and section it out along with some roasted veggies for the week.

203. Salad with a savory twist. Precook burger patties and then crumble them over your lunchtime salads to make delicious "burger bowls."

204. Pasta salad. A cold pasta salad can be premade in bulk with a variety of veggie and protein options you have on hand. Enjoy right out of the fridge!

205. Smoothies. Freeze bags of sliced and portioned mixed fruit and blend up your healthy lunch in a flash.

206. Stuffed peppers. This delicious option can be made in no time with your favorite ingredients and then reheated when it's time to eat.

207. A homemade version of a frozen favorite. Almost every popular frozen food has a homemade equivalent. Consider making your own pizza pockets, chicken nuggets, or other favorite. You'll have a much healthier option, without losing any of the flavor!

208. Group personal appointments toward the beginning or end of the day so they don't disrupt your workday. When you have a flexible schedule, it's easy to think that it doesn't really matter when you plan things like doctor's appointments, but it does. If you wouldn't leave the office in the middle of the day to get your teeth cleaned, then don't leave your home office to do it either.

209. Match work schedules with your coworkers. If everyone in your office works in New York while you're the only employee in Los Angeles, consider shifting your workday to match that of your coworkers. When you work at a different time than others in your office, it can be difficult to resolve issues and communicate in a timely manner. While there certainly are some positions where it makes sense to have people working separate shifts, if your job isn't one of them, look into ways that you and your coworkers can overlap your schedules.

210. **Keep an extra set of batteries handy.** Without fail, the batteries in your keyboard or computer mouse will run out while you're in the middle of working on something with a tight deadline. Having an extra set of batteries on hand ensures that you don't get stuck in a situation where you have to run to the store in the middle of the day when you really need to be working on a project.

211. **Stay connected with a coworker via video chat during the day.** If you're working on a large project with another person, consider putting yourselves in a constant video chat during the workday, especially if your coworker also works from home. By using video chat, you can easily ask questions and communicate with that person just as if you were working with him in a traditional office. Even better, you'll also be able to physically see that the person has walked away for lunch or to use the restroom, so you won't have to wonder why he is not responding to a question or concern you've raised.

212. **Participate in happy hour.** Scheduling a happy hour meetup with friends or coworkers for the end of the workday can serve two great purposes. First, it will get you out of the house and talking to other humans (something you likely haven't done much of during the day). Second, if you have a happy hour scheduled for six p.m., you'll have a motivating reason for getting all of your work done by that time.

213. **Send your boss an end-of-the-week update.** While it's great not to have your boss looking over your shoulder all day, she also doesn't really know how you spent your time. Let your boss know on a weekly basis what you've accomplished during the week and what you hope to complete the following week. Not only does this force you to get things done (who wants to tell her boss that she did nothing?), but it also confirms that you and your boss are always on the same page about the work you're doing.

214. Even if it's biweekly, schedule regular video meetings with those you work with as a way to collaborate, to keep in touch with them and their projects, and to let them know about how you're doing. It's a great way to still feel like you're part of the team, even remotely!

☑ ☑ ☑

215. Complete stressful tasks outside of your home. When you're exceptionally stressed, you're more susceptible to getting distracted from your work. It's like having a "fight or flight" response: you'll be susceptible to going into "flight" mode and toward doing your dishes or mopping the kitchen floor. If you take stressful tasks somewhere else, you'll be able to work on them with fewer distractions, and you won't associate your home with that stress.

216. **Practice prolonged concentration.** You can train yourself to work for prolonged periods of time without getting distracted by things around the house. Start by working for thirty minutes at a time with a five-minute break, then scale that time up in ten-minute increments until you're able to work for two hours or more without interruption. During the training portion, set an alarm on your phone to let you know when your time is up. While those thirty minutes might seem painful at first, once you've trained yourself to handle longer periods of time, you won't know how doing so was ever a problem.

217. **Move someplace where there isn't an Internet connection to distract you.** Coffee shops that don't have Wi-Fi can be the perfect place to hunker down and finish a report or get some reading done that you can't seem to focus on at home. While working from the bar isn't the best idea on a regular basis, spending one afternoon a week working with a low-alcohol beer or a cocktail (or mocktail!) at your local watering hole can be just the change of pace you need to get things done while feeling like you're getting some relaxation in as well.

218. Pick a time that is the official "end" to your day and force yourself to "go home" just as if you were leaving the traditional office. Don't put yourself in a position where you're working all the time just because you can. Sure, you might not have finished everything you had hoped to accomplish for the day, but that would have happened at a traditional office as well. Separate your work and personal life, and allow yourself to leave your home office when you're supposed to do so. Just because your home is your office doesn't mean you need to act like you're always on the job.

219. Schedule social posts to go out over several hours. If social media is a part of your business or daily life, scheduling posts rather than posting manually allows you to walk away from distracting websites for a few hours and focus on other tasks.

END-OF-DAY TASKS TO KEEP YOU ORGANIZED

Nothing can destroy your productivity quite like disorganization. Try to devote a few minutes at the end of each workday to ensure that your workspace is organized and you're set up for success the next morning. Here are some things to do at the end of the day to keep you organized:

220. Make sure you have caught up with your inbox. If you still have emails you need to respond to in the morning, put them in an appropriate folder or "snooze" them so that they'll be at the top of the to-do list in the morning.

221. Put away any stray papers and files that are left on your desk.

222. Restock any office supplies you might have used up during the day, such as pencils, pens, or Post-it notes.

223. Double-check your calendar to make sure you've added any new items that came up during the day.

224. Get rid of any empty water bottles and dirty coffee cups you might have left on your desk.

225. Create a short to-do list of items you hope to accomplish first thing in the morning so they're at the top of your mind when you get back to your desk.

226. Plug in your laptop and make sure any other electronics you used during the day are charged and back where they belong.

227. Turn off anything that runs on a battery, such as your computer's mouse or keyboard.

228. Clean out your office trash so you don't end up in a situation where it needs to be emptied while you're busy working on something the next day.

229. Review your calendar and set up any alarms you might need to remember events or tasks the following day.

CHAPTER 4

PRODUCTIVE BUSINESS TRAVEL

230. **Take the first flight of the day to your destination.** There are a ton of benefits to nabbing that first flight. The airport is likely a bit less congested, so you can enjoy shorter lines everywhere from security to Starbucks. Early flights are also less likely to be delayed because the planes are already at the airport and the crew is fresh. If your early flight does get delayed, then you know that your flight will still be the first one out to your destination.

231. **Carry a small power strip.** Power outlets in airport terminals are notoriously scarce. Guarantee that you'll always be able to charge your stuff by keeping a power strip with you. Something small with just two or three plugs can easily slip into a laptop bag. It can also come in handy if your hotel room doesn't have quite enough outlets to charge your tech.

232. **Schedule meetings around your flight.** When you let the meeting dictate your flight, you often end up taking a flight at an inconvenient time that throws off your schedule and productivity elsewhere. While it won't work for every situation, find the flight that fits within your schedule best and then set up your meetings around that flight rather than the other way around. If you're the one setting the meeting, then it makes sense for it to be at a time that works best for you.

✓ ✓ ✓

233. **Buy a set of toiletries and other essentials to keep in your suitcase if you travel for work often.** Is there anything more frustrating than getting to your destination only to discover you've left behind your toothbrush, hairbrush, or razor? If you have duplicates of your essentials that live in your suitcase, you won't accidentally leave any of them at home. If you're always traveling to your company's headquarters elsewhere, consider buying full-sized versions of your essentials and leaving them at your remote office so they're already there when you visit and you don't have to tote things back and forth.

THINGS YOU NEED IN YOUR CARRY-ON

Your carry-on is going to be with you for the duration of your flight, so it's important to pack the things that will make your trip go smoothly. Here are a few essential things to pack in your carry-on:

234. A backup battery to keep your phone charged during your trip if the plane you're on doesn't have power outlets.

235. Mindless entertainment. Whether it's a game or a downloaded movie, having something to do to take your mind off work for a bit will be a welcome distraction, and it will give your mind a break so you're ready to hit the ground running when you land.

236. Printed reading material (a.k.a. that work-related reading you've been putting off). This will be a great way to spend that time during takeoff and before you land when you're not allowed to use electronics.

237. An inflatable pillow. Airplane seats are notoriously uncomfortable. An inflatable neck pillow can add a layer of comfort to your trip without weighing you down, and it can be deflated for easy packing when you're done with it. Never underestimate the energizing power of an in-flight nap!

238. An eye mask so you can still enjoy a snooze when the person sitting in the window seat decides he wants to look outside.

239. Earplugs to drown out that screaming baby or chatterbox in the seat behind you.

240. Aspirin. Especially on planes, it's easy for a headache to come on. Save yourself the pain by having relief in your bag.

241. A small pack of antiseptic wipes to wipe down your seat, entertainment console, and tray table when you sit down. While airline crews clean planes between flights, they don't typically wipe down surfaces. You don't know if the last occupant of your seat was battling the flu, a stomach virus, or worse. Nothing kills productivity like catching the flu.

242. A water bottle. Flying on planes is dehydrating. Fill the bottle up at a water fountain before you get on your flight. Hydration is key to staying focused and productive!

243. A change of clothes. Delays happen and bags get lost. Keep an outfit in your carry-on just in case you run into trouble so you're not left scrambling for something to wear when you land.

244. **Download the app for the airline you're traveling with.** The airline's app can be your portal to moving to a more preferable seat and keeping track of what gate you're supposed to go to. It can also be your first line of defense when it comes to finding out whether or not your flight has been delayed. In many cases, you can even check in to your flight and get a digital version of your boarding pass so you don't have to stop at the check-in desk.

245. **Fly in the night before if you have a morning meeting.** Even if your office is willing to spring for only one night in a hotel, staying in town the night before a big meeting is a lot less stressful than trying to catch a flight at the crack of dawn in order to get to the meeting on time. If you fly in the night before, you'll be well rested and on time for your meeting.

246. **Avoid checking a bag at the airport.** Nothing slows you down when you're trying to leave the airport like picking up a checked bag. Checking a bag means that you'll have to wait at the baggage carousel to reclaim it before you can leave the airport, and it introduces the opportunity of having your bag lost somewhere during your travels. You avoid a lot of unnecessary trouble by simply keeping your bag with you.

✓ ✓ ✓

247. **Call the airline directly about flight issues.** When a flight gets severely delayed or canceled, most airline help desks wind up getting immediately overrun by passengers trying to change their travel plans. While the airport staff can certainly be helpful, the pro move is to contact the airline call center. Someone at the airline's call center can often rebook you on another flight faster than if you wait in a long line—which could mean the difference between getting the last seat on the next flight and getting stranded where you are.

248. **Wear something to the airport that you would be comfortable wearing to a business meeting.** Flights can be unpredictable, and you never know when your flight might be unexpectedly delayed. If you're already dressed for your meeting when you board, it won't be an issue if you need to take a cab right to your meeting rather than to your hotel when you land.

249. **Opt for snazzy luggage.** Yes, a simple black suitcase looks great, but everyone else thinks so too, so finding yours on the baggage carousel (if you have to check it) can potentially turn into a nightmare. Make your luggage easy to find by purchasing a suitcase in a unique color or with a unique design, or by using a brightly colored luggage tag. You'll be able to see your bag coming on the carousel more easily, and others will be deterred from accidentally removing your bag thinking it's their own.

250. **Use TSA PreCheck.** Even for infrequent fliers, TSA PreCheck is a solid investment. In TSA PreCheck, the TSA does a background search on you prior to your flight to determine if you're a potential threat. Once you're at the airport, you're able to go through a shorter security line where you're not required to take off your shoes, remove electronics from your bag, or walk through a body scanner. The PreCheck line also moves faster since there are fewer instructions to follow and it's made up of mostly frequent fliers.

✓ ✓ ✓

251. **If you are traveling internationally, Global Entry is a huge time saver.** The program allows US citizens, as well as citizens from a number of other countries, to enter or reenter the United States through a short line and skip filling out paper customs forms. Instead, you answer the questions on the customs form at a kiosk when you land and scan your fingerprints. When you do, you get a printout to show the customs agent so you can breeze on through the line.

252. **Buy a TSA-approved carry-on bag.** If you don't have TSA PreCheck, make sure you're using a bag that makes it simple to take out things like electronics and toiletries during the security check. This kind of bag often just needs to be unzipped at security and doesn't require you to physically remove items, so you can move quickly through the line and have time for a preflight coffee.

253. **Roll your clothes rather than fold them.** When you're packing your suitcase, rolling clothes will prevent them from getting wrinkled during your travels and will save you time when you get to your destination since you won't have to iron anything. If your clothes do get lightly wrinkled, hang them up in the bathroom when you take a shower to let the steam remove at least some of the wrinkles.

254. **Upgrade to priority boarding.** Priority boarding will allow you to get on the plane earlier than most of the other travelers (when flying economy), ensuring that you find a spot for your bag in the overhead bin so you won't be required to check it. Some airlines also offer the ability to get priority service at the check-in desk, which can help you skip the long line and prevent you from missing your flight if you happen to arrive at the airport late.

255. **Research the airports you are flying from and any places you stop over.** While small airports are simple enough to navigate, larger airports can get exceptionally complicated. Knowing that you'll need to catch a train to another terminal during your layover can cut down on stress and confusion during a tight connection. You'll also want to have an idea of what to do when you land. For instance, if you plan on taking a cab when you arrive, know where those pickup locations are ahead of time, especially when you have a meeting to get to.

WAYS TO BE PRODUCTIVE ON AN AIRPLANE

Flying is one of those rare times when you're able to sit completely uninterrupted for a long period. Even if you don't have "work" to accomplish while you're in the air, there are a number of things you can do to make your flight a productive one, with or without Wi-Fi:

256. Clean up your email inbox, or draft responses to emails you haven't had time to respond to.

257. Clean up the files on your computer, and make sure everything is in its rightful place.

258. Create a list of goals for your business trip and what you would like to accomplish.

259. Delete phone contacts you no longer need. While you do, take note of people you haven't spoken to in a while and plan to connect with them via email or calls in the coming weeks.

260. Chat for a few minutes with your neighbor. Don't hog her time, but given that you're both headed the same way, you might have a business-related connection worth exploring.

261. Mentally rehearse your conference speech, meeting objectives, or anticipated business conversations.

262. Think through an issue that you've recently found challenging at work, and brainstorm a few solutions to revisit once you return.

263. Think about your goals for the year, and come up with a list of high-level goals for what you'd like to accomplish in your professional and personal life.

264. Finally read that inspirational book you bought months ago.

265. Organize your workbag. If your bag was a mess when you boarded, take the time in-flight to organize everything so you can start fresh when you land.

266. Stick to your normal time zone at your destination instead of trying to adapt to a different time zone. Switching time zones can be brutal on your body and can lead to sleepy days and nights when you're wide awake. For instance, if you live in New York but are spending a few days in San Francisco, still work your "normal" shift and try to schedule meetings within that time frame. You might not be able to keep exactly the same schedule, but the closer you can get, the more productive your trip will be.

267. Prepare work materials for possible Wi-Fi issues. While most airlines offer Wi-Fi these days, it always seems like the one time you're counting on using it to work during your trip is when something is wrong with it. Before you fly, make sure you have everything you need to get your work done downloaded to your computer and available to access offline—that way if the Internet is down on your plane, your productivity won't take a hit. This means things like setting up your browser and email client to offline mode so you can access pages and your messages without connectivity.

268. Bring a good pair of noise-canceling head-phones. Screaming babies and chatty seat-mates are not exactly conducive to getting work done. Noise-canceling headphones can help you drown out what's going on around you and focus on the important task in front of you (even if that important task just happens to be a power nap). If you don't have any head-phones, a pair of earplugs can work in a pinch and make your flying experience significantly more enjoyable.

✓ ✓ ✓

269. Add a wireless hot spot feature to your phone. While the feature may add a small extra expense to your mobile bill, having a hot spot means you'll have a data connection to check email and communicate with work when you need to, and you won't have to scramble to find a local coffee shop or ask around for a Wi-Fi password.

270. **Always pack things in the same place.** There's nothing worse than getting to your destination and not being able to find something you need. By creating a system for where everything is packed, you'll be able to find things much more easily when you need them.

271. **Know the Wi-Fi situation at a hotel before you book it.** Search through the hotel's reviews to see how previous guests have felt about the Wi-Fi. Internet quality can vary dramatically from hotel to hotel; even hotels in big cities might not offer Wi-Fi in their rooms, or if they do, that Internet connection might be expensive. If you plan on working in your hotel room, you don't want to struggle with a slow connection or have to tote your work down to the lobby to get a strong signal.

272.

Log out of your company's chat programs on your phone while you're on the road. You're traveling for a reason, so don't get caught up in what's going on in the office while you're away. The office will still be there when you get back, but you have only one shot at doing what you're traveling for. If someone back home really needs you for a pressing issue, he can contact you via text or phone call.

273. **Watch the labels!** Airlines can get sneaky when they label flights. This especially comes into play with "direct" and "nonstop" flights. A direct flight is one that will fly to your destination but will make stops along the way. You'll stay on the same plane, but you'll have to wait for some people to get off and get on at those pit stops. What you want is a nonstop flight, which flies directly to your destination with no interruptions and is significantly faster.

✓ ✓ ✓

274. **Charge everything you can before you head to the airport.** You never know when an outlet might be out of service or when the power might go out.

275. **Order the vegetarian option.** Vegetarian meals and meals for people with food allergies are often served before the meals for the rest of the plane. That means you'll be able to finish your meal and move on to other tasks, in some cases before the rest of your row even gets served. Eating a lighter, healthier meal will also help you focus on your work while you fly.

276. **Use packing cubes to keep your suitcase organized.** Use the cubes to separate shoes from clothes and to keep socks and underwear organized while adding very little weight to your overall luggage. Even better, cubes also keep dirty clothes separated from the rest of your items when your travel home.

277. **Use offline time to get organized.** Offline time on a plane or train is a great time to fine-tune your to-do list for the trip or clean up a cluttered desktop on your laptop.

278. **If you have a long layover, buy access to the airline's lounge.** Airline lounges have places to sit down and work, decent free Wi-Fi, and free drinks and food. If you plan on working through that layover, then the cost is worth it to be sure that you won't be wandering around the airport looking for something to eat and a decent place to sit. Some airline lounges also offer showers where you can freshen up for that meeting you have to get to after you land.

279.

While Google Maps won't show any real-time traffic information, you can have it save an offline view of a city. Even in situations where you don't have a cell signal, this view can help you determine where your hotel is in relation to a restaurant where you're meeting coworkers or give you directions to walk back to the hotel after a trip to a bar.

280. **Set an "out of office" reply to let people know you're on the road.** Regardless of your email access, your schedule while traveling is destined to be different from your schedule while you're at the office. By setting an "out of office" message you're letting people know that your schedule might be a little out of the norm. If you're in an entirely different time zone or know you won't be responding to email, make sure you give people another option, such as calling you on the phone or emailing a coworker to handle their issue. This will ensure that issues get resolved quickly and potentially without your involvement—and you won't have to waste time explaining that you're out of town to everyone who contacts you.

✓ ✓ ✓

281. **Keep a piece of paper on you with the name and number of your hotel and the address of your business event.** Accidents happen, and if your phone gets lost, broken, or stolen during your trip, you'll be hugging yourself for having that note. Even better, print out your schedule to carry with you as well.

282. **Download the AirHelp app.** If you run into delays or other airline issues when you fly, AirHelp will file a compensation claim for you with the airline—all you have to do is input your ticket information! With a few clicks, the dirty work is done for you in no time.

✓ ✓ ✓

283. **Make an itinerary.** If you're headed to a large conference, make sure to plan what sessions you'd like to attend before you arrive, not when you're already there. You'll also want to pay attention to where the sessions are located. If you want to attend two things that are at the same time, you'll need to pick one or the other before you go. Don't miss out on something simply due to poor planning. And the same goes for business trips: having a good idea of where you want to go, how far away events are, and how you plan to get around will make your travels go much more smoothly.

284. **Pick a hotel that's close to your business event.** Commuting when you're at home is hard enough—save yourself the trouble when you're on a business trip. Even if there's another hotel that's slightly cheaper across town, think about the money and time you'll save when you don't have to commute back and forth.

285. **Traveling for a larger event like a conference?** Check your phone—there may be an app for that! A conference app will have the full schedule for the event as well as a map of the conference location to help you get around. Even better, organizers often use the app to send out updates on everything from session changes to where a surprise happy hour is being held.

286. **Don't use a business trip to try out a new pair of shoes or outfit.** While it might be nice to wear a fancy new suit to that meeting, it can quickly become an epic nightmare if the fabric itches or it is too small. Since you're away from home when those new shoes start giving you blisters, you won't have anything to change into. Stick with clothing you already know and love when you travel so you aren't stuck trying to find new clothes before a meeting or focusing on your aching feet during an important presentation.

☑ ☑ ☑

287. **Room service might seem like a luxury, but it can actually be an efficient way to eat while you're on the road, especially for breakfast.** Having room service deliver will force you to wake up and be ready at that time, and you'll skip out on the long, chaotic lines in the dining room.

288. **Most nicer hotels offer laundry services for guests.** If you're traveling from one business destination to another, bring fewer clothes and have the hotel at your first destination do laundry for you before you head to your second destination. Carrying a smaller bag can help prevent having to check a bag or carrying something bulky around from destination to destination. The service also saves you the time in having to do your laundry when you get home.

289. **Turn your phone off to conserve battery power during your flight.** Leaving your phone on during the flight, especially if you forget to put it in airplane mode, will drain your battery. Turning your phone off certifies that you have a full battery when you land for catching up on emails, responding to text messages, and calling a car service to get you to your hotel.

290. **Ask the hotel to give you a wake-up call.** Even if you set the alarm on your phone, it's way too easy for you to run into a mishap where you set it for the wrong time or your phone runs out of juice because you didn't plug it in properly in the unfamiliar outlet. A wake-up call from the hotel will make sure that you wake up when you need to.

✓ ✓ ✓

291. **Immediately snap pictures of your receipts.** If your company's expense tracking software has a mobile version, you can input the expense right after you make it. Not only will this save you time when you return home, but it will also ensure you don't lose a receipt between the purchase and when you fill out your expense report.

292. **Save your foreign currency.** When you exchange money from one currency to another, you not only lose a little bit of money on each end, but you also waste your time standing in line at the exchange counter. While it isn't exactly practical to keep thousands of dollars in foreign currencies in your possession, if you have any spending money left over after a trip and think you may revisit that location, save it. Not only will you save yourself from taking the hit when you make the exchange, but you'll also be sure that you have cash on hand from the moment you land during your next trip.

293. **Pack some nonperishable snacks for the plane and your hotel room.** Nothing can slow you down like being hungry. Something as small as a package of trail mix can be a magical thing to have on hand when you're working late and need a little pick-me-up, or when you're on a flight where the crew just serves pretzels and you need something a little more substantial.

294. **Get to bed at a reasonable hour.** Work trips, especially group ones, can often lead to long nights out at the bar or work-related mixers with colleagues. Staying out late can certainly be fun, but trying to make it through the next day without a full night of sleep won't be. While it's great to make an appearance at these events, avoid being part of the group that shuts the bar down.

295. **Take a vitamin C supplement before you fly.** People aren't really productive when they're sick. Traveling even a short distance can take its toll on your body, and planes often put you in close proximity to someone who isn't feeling well. In addition to getting enough sleep and drinking plenty of water, up your vitamin C intake to fight off any germs that come your way.

APPS EVERY TRAVELER SHOULD DOWNLOAD

When you're traveling away from home, the apps on your phone can be a great way to stay organized and connected, and to make sure your travels are as pleasant as they can be. Here are a few apps that every business traveler should have:

296. Not all airplane seats are created equal. SeatGuru will help you pick the perfect seat on the plane so you don't end up stuck in an uncomfortable spot where it's hard to work or sleep during your trip.

297. If you're not already a member of an airport lounge, LoungeBuddy can score you access to one at the airport for as little as $25. Airport lounges can offer you access to fast Internet to do a little work, outlets to charge your gear, and snacks to keep you energized.

298. When we create our own packing checklists, we often forget a few things—sometimes things we didn't even realize we needed in the first place. PackPoint looks at the weather at your destination and asks what you plan on doing during your trip, then it creates a personalized checklist of what you should bring so you don't leave any necessary items behind!

299. If you need to find your way around a new city, Citymapper is just the ticket. This app helps you find the fastest way to your destination and can let you know when you need to get off a bus or train.

300. Find a Wi-Fi hot spot when you need it using WiFi Map. This app not only shares where hot spots are but also provides the password for them in many cases.

301. When you're driving in a new place, use Waze. This app offers real-time traffic information and alerts you to hazards like potholes, roadkill, accidents, and more.

302. Sometimes work trips are unexpected. HotelTonight offers great same-day deals on hotel rooms. In most cases you can stay at five-star hotels for a fraction of what you would pay on the hotel's website.

303. TripIt organizes all of your travel plans into a single location. As you receive travel information like hotel and flight info, just forward it to your TripIt address!

304. When you travel to a foreign country, Duolingo can be an easy way for you to learn a little bit of the language before you arrive. Even playing just a few of the app's educational games on the plane will help you learn some of the basics before you land. If you know even a little bit of the native language, getting around and communicating will be much easier.

305. Go on the perfect run at your destination using RunGo. The app suggests safe and interesting running routes near you and offers voice navigation when you set out on your journey. That way you can save time searching for the perfect spot and just hit the road—and get yourself energized for that afternoon meeting!

306. **Scout out where your meeting is and the best way to get there ahead of time.** People don't want to be late to something they've traveled so far to get to. Set yourself up for success by figuring things out beforehand. When it comes time for that meeting, you'll be on time—not out of breath. And you may even have time to grab a cup of coffee on the way.

307. **Ship larger items.** Having a lot of luggage will slow you down at the airport. Instead, send any big packages ahead of you to your destination. They will be there when you arrive, and you won't have to wait for them at the baggage carousel or figure out how to haul them from the airport to your hotel once you land.

CHAPTER 5

HAVING PRODUCTIVE MEETINGS

308. **Evaluate why you chose to meet in the first place.** It's easy to fall into the habit of having a meeting on a specific day or at a specific time just because you always do, not because the meeting is really necessary. Identify the main objective of the meeting first. If you are having trouble coming up with a truly good reason to meet, discuss canceling the meeting so everyone can spend that time on something more productive.

☑ ☑ ☑

309. **Choose the right way to get together for a particular meeting.** If you're just getting to know a client or having your first meeting with someone, an in-person meeting is a great way to go. But if you're having a meeting to just touch base or go over a few details of a project with people you work with regularly, consider having a phone meeting. While the actual length of your meeting might not change, a phone meeting can cut down on everyone's commute time to that meeting. Stay put when you can—you'll thank yourself later when you can use that time saved from not traveling for finishing up other projects.

310. **Group your meetings outside of the office together.** Rather than traveling to the same area and back to your office multiple times in the same day or week, scheduling these meetings together will cut down on the amount of time you have to spend traveling. If you have frequent meetings outside of the office, having a dedicated "out of office" day for meetings can come in handy.

☑ ☑ ☑

311. **Make sure everyone who *needs* to be there *can* be there.** There's no point in having a meeting if all the key players can't make it or if a major stakeholder will have to arrive late or leave early. Don't get stuck in a meeting where you have to make a note to "check on that with Bob" a half dozen times. Make sure Bob is able to be there so he can contribute in the moment.

QUESTIONS TO ASK YOURSELF BEFORE SCHEDULING A MEETING

Before you send out meeting invites, make sure you know all of the general information, from why you are having the meeting to how you can ensure that everyone's voice is heard. Here are a few key questions to ask yourself before you schedule that meeting:

312. Why do I want to have this meeting?

313. Could this meeting be handled in an email?

314. What goal am I trying to achieve by the end of the meeting?

315. How can I make this meeting useful for all attendees?

316. Who absolutely needs to attend this meeting? Do those people need to stay the entire time?

317. What information can I provide before the meeting to make it run easier?

318. How can I organize the meeting so everyone's voice is heard?

319. How long does the meeting really need to be to achieve my goal?

320. What's a convenient time to meet with this particular group of people?

321. How can I guarantee that all attendees leave with specific tasks to handle once the meeting is over?

322. **Think about whether or not you can accomplish the same task over email or in a group chat.** A large percentage of in-person meetings are simply to recap the previous day's tasks, or to discuss or accomplish tasks that could have been handled in just a few minutes in a group chat or short email chain. You definitely don't want to replace a meeting with twenty emails, but if it could be accomplished in four emails or less, you'll save everyone a bit of time by switching things to a digital conversation.

323. **Start every meeting by stating its point to the group.** Even though everyone might know they're there to discuss a particular project, they may have different thoughts about what specifically is being covered in that meeting. By stating your goal to the group, you're ensuring that everyone is on the same page. You can also answer questions like "Will graphics be covered in this meeting?" so that people know what to expect and don't interrupt with off-topic questions or comments later.

324. **Create an agenda.** If you're the one scheduling the meeting, one of the most important things you can do to prep is to give everyone a meeting agenda. An agenda keeps everyone on the same page as to what specifically is going to be discussed and in what order.

325. **When you start a meeting, set a timer that rings when the meeting is scheduled to end.** Just knowing that the timer is there is often enough to push things along. If you have several agenda items to get through, you can also set the timer to ring when each discussion should be complete.

326. **Compile a "required reading" list.** Rather than waste time in a meeting listening to people give updates on where they are in a project, ask everyone to email you their updates. You can then create a single document that is sent out to all of the attendees prior to the meeting. People can read everything before they arrive, and the group can spend the meeting answering questions and working out finer points rather than getting hung up on long updates.

327. **Tailor your attendee list to include only the people who need to be part of the decision-making conversation.** People don't want to spend time in a meeting that they don't need to be in. Having extra people in a meeting opens the discussion up to off-topic conversations and eats into the time that those people could be using to get their actual work done. Instead, if a person's role in the meeting could be replaced by an email or a short phone call before or after, do that instead.

328.

Establish why your attendance is important. If you're not the one hosting a meeting but you receive an invite from a colleague, ask why you need to be there. If there's a compelling reason for you to attend, your colleague will be able to explain why she thinks your attendance will add to the meeting. If she can't provide a reason for you being there, suggest that you skip it. Attending a meeting where you're not needed is a waste of your time and will make the meeting less efficient in the long run.

329. **Always start your meetings on time.** When you wait for stragglers, you're telling the people who did arrive on time that you don't value their time as much as you value the time of those late attendees. When you're known for starting meetings on time, people will make an effort to be there at the correct time instead of dragging in five or ten minutes later—so you can get down to business.

330. **Ask people to write down any questions they have at the beginning of the meeting.** Saving the question portion of the meeting until the end is the fast track to a long meeting. Hopefully you already planned to address the questions people wrote down. If not, you can incorporate answers into your existing meeting rather than tacking them on at the end. If you're holding a longer meeting, consider having a question section in the middle of the meeting as well to off-load any new questions.

331. **Identify all action items at the end of the meeting.** This rundown makes sure everyone is on the same page and has a clear idea of what their next tasks are.

332. **Turn a one-on-one meeting into a walking meeting.** Going on a walk can give you both the opportunity to leave the office for a few minutes and get some exercise. The act of walking will get your blood flowing and stimulate your brain, encouraging more creative solutions to problems than you might have thought of in a windowless conference room.

TIPS FOR BEING AN ACTIVE LISTENER IN A MEETING

The entire point of attending a meeting is to pay attention to the speaker. But depending on the speaker, sometimes that's easier said than done. Here are a couple of easy tips for being an active listener in a meeting and getting the most out of your attendance:

333. Avoid looking at other attendees, your laptop, or your notes while the presentation is happening. Put your computer and unrelated notes away.

334. If you find your attention drifting, repeat the meeting topic in your head five times to bring yourself back to the task at hand.

335. Observe the speaker's body language to determine what that can add to what he is saying. If your boss seems particularly excited about one aspect of a project, that's a good indication you should be excited about it too and should perhaps prioritize that element over others.

336. Even though you might have feedback or a rebuttal to what's being discussed, don't mentally prepare your statements while the speaker is still talking. Listen.

337. Maintain good posture throughout the presentation, and avoid slouching in your chair. Slouching can give the impression that you're not paying attention when you are, and it can lead your brain into "relax mode."

338. Nod occasionally throughout the presentation to let the speaker know that you're interested in what she has to say and that you agree with a particular point. Beyond letting her know you're listening, it can also help her feel encouraged so she'll move the meeting along.

339. Hold all your questions until the end of a presentation to confirm you have all the facts before you make a comment. When you interrupt a speaker, you slow the whole meeting down and can throw everything off track—especially if your question was going to be answered by the speaker as part of the presentation.

340. Before criticizing an idea, start with an "I" statement, such as "I understood you to say X," acknowledging that you may have misheard or not fully understood the idea. The statement avoids upsetting the speaker and instead frames your comment as an explanation, allowing him to clarify any issues so you can ask more informed questions.

341. Don't be afraid to ask for the speaker to clarify certain points once she's done speaking. If you don't understand what was discussed in the meeting, you will be wasting your time—and the speaker's.

342. Don't interrupt others. Pay attention to someone's full remarks before making your own. Talking over others can slow down the pace of a meeting and even derail it. Give people a chance to say their piece!

343. Avoid setting a meeting for "brainstorming." Brainstorming is something that people can do individually, and group brainstorming sessions can quickly get off track, as there is no clear direction. Instead of doing the brainstorming in a meeting, have everyone come up with a list of ideas on their own to send to you. Compile the best ideas and then use a meeting time to discuss only those ideas and how to execute them.

344. Address obstacles at the beginning of the meeting (yes, even if they are uncomfortable). If you're dancing around the elephant in the room, you're eating away valuable discussion time. By acknowledging a big issue like budget concerns or staffing issues at the onset, you can incorporate it into your solutions instead of pretending it doesn't exist.

345. Use *NeedToMeet* for larger meetings. If you're trying to schedule a meeting that involves a number of different people, finding a time that works for everyone is a challenge. NeedToMeet.com allows you as a meeting organizer to propose a few meeting times and then have attendees note which of those options work best for them.

346. Stick to five (or fewer) specific agenda items. When your meeting is overloaded with topics, you'll either have a *very* long meeting or won't be able to give every topic the attention it deserves. If you find that a meeting needs to have more than five agenda items, consider whether any of those could be addressed before or after the meeting, or with individuals directly rather than in front of the entire group. If you really need the group of people for more than five topics, break the discussion up into two meetings if possible.

347.

Have your meetings in the after-noon. You may think that setting a morning meeting means everyone will arrive ready to hit the ground running—but actually you may just end up with a meeting full of people who got caught up with work the day before and consequently didn't have time to prepare. An afternoon meeting—specifically in the middle of the week—will result in a more engaged and better-prepared group than if you had the same meeting at nine a.m. on a Monday when people are still recovering from the weekend and catching up on work they didn't finish the week before.

348. **Hold creative meetings outdoors.** You still want to find a spot where your group won't be interrupted, but having a change of scenery from the regular office space can spark creativity and lead to a much more engaged meeting.

☑ ☑ ☑

349. **Ask yourself if the answer to your question will be helpful to everyone in the group or just you.** If you're in a ten-person meeting and have a question that applies only to you personally, perhaps the large group setting isn't the right place to ask. Instead, wait until the meeting is over, and approach the organizer on your own with your query. Respect the time of others—you may even find you are influencing them to do the same.

350. **Book the conference room for fifteen minutes before the meeting is scheduled to start and fifteen minutes after it's supposed to end.** Sometimes meetings run late. The beginning buffer gives the people who were in the room before you time to clear out so you don't have to wait for them, and it makes sure that your meeting attendees can get in the room and get settled before the meeting starts.

✓ ✓ ✓

351. **Schedule your meetings for an appropriate amount of time.** People tend to default to set periods of time (like one hour) when holding meetings, when in fact most meetings could be handled in much less time. If your meeting agenda will take only fifteen minutes but you've scheduled the meeting for an hour, the meeting itself will likely be filled with a lot of small talk and unproductive conversations. Instead, schedule your meeting for the shortest amount of time you think you'll need to accomplish your goal. When the meeting is only fifteen minutes, attendees are much more likely to arrive on time and stay focused.

352. **Opt to have meetings longer than thirty minutes in person rather than over a conference call.** People who are dialed into a conference line could also be surfing *Facebook*, cooking breakfast, or even walking their dogs. While some people can actively listen and simultaneously do something else, most can't. Guarantee that you have an engaged audience for the meeting by holding it in person instead.

353. **Before every meeting pick someone to serve as the meeting's monitor to keep everyone on topic.** That person shouldn't be the meeting organizer since the organizer is likely to be one of the people who speaks longer than necessary on a topic. The monitor's role in the meeting is to keep track of time and confirm that the meeting is progressing on schedule and staying on topic. If someone proposes an off-topic discussion, the monitor can add the discussion point to a list to be addressed after the meeting's agenda has been satisfied or at a subsequent meeting.

354. Once you've created a meeting agenda and sent it out to attendees, be prepared to stick to that agenda and only that agenda when the meeting actually begins, and make sure everyone else attending the meeting knows that's the plan as well. It's easy to get off track in meetings, which can make them last longer or, even worse, means that you need to schedule another meeting to actually accomplish what you intended to do in the first one. Consider the agenda written in stone and reiterate that to all attendees when the meeting begins.

✓ ✓ ✓

355. Welcome different opinions. If there's someone in your office who feels differently about a task than you do, invite him to the meeting. While it might seem counterintuitive to have someone who disagrees with you present, that person's presence can lead to a much more balanced discussion. And since you're including the person in the decision-making process, you'll also cut down on the possibility of conflicts with him in the future.

356. **Disperse the more outspoken people through-out the meeting room.** Every office has a few people who are more vocal than others. If you place those people close to the meeting organizer, the rest of the room can easily seem more excluded from the discussion. Instead, space out those attendees throughout the room to create an environment where everyone feels comfortable speaking.

357. **Provide a "six-pager" document.** Created by Amazon executives, the six-pager provides all of the background and context that people will need to understand the proposal, design, or update being discussed. This way easy questions like "What does this acronym mean?" won't need to be asked in the middle of the conversation. The six-pager is especially great when you're going over a more complex topic.

358. **Check in with folks who haven't yet said much—or anything—in the meeting.** This is especially true for remote workers—make sure they have a chance to chime in! If they're there, it must be because their presence is valued and they have something to bring to the table in that discussion.

✓ ✓ ✓

359. **Make sure all meeting attendees have a reason to show up on time.** Nothing derails a meeting like a key attendee showing up late. Not only do you have to stop the meeting, but you also have to repeat a lot of what's already happened. One easy way to ensure everyone's on time is to have a negative consequence for showing up late. The consequence can be something simple, like requiring the last person who arrives at the meeting to be responsible for taking meeting notes, or something more complex, like giving that person the last pick of assignments for the next big project.

360. **Require everyone to keep their phones and laptops tucked away.** Phones and computers are essential to getting work done, but they're also huge distractions. Having an electronics-free meeting will keep everyone on task and prevent people from getting distracted by instant messages, emails, and texts that don't pertain to the meeting.

361. **Keep food out of the room.** Snacks always seem like a great idea at meetings, but they never are. While offering doughnuts from that bakery around the corner is an easy way to make sure people show up to a meeting, it's also a quick way to guarantee that the first ten minutes of the meeting are spent with people selecting the perfect doughnuts and eating them. If you want to keep your meeting fast and on topic, don't offer food and ask others not to bring their own.

362. When you schedule a meeting (even a casual one), send a meeting invite. A calendar invite will hold the space on people's schedules and remind them about your discussion to have the meeting in the first place. When you don't send an invite, you're counting on people to remember your conversation and add the meeting to their calendars on their own. They might remember, but the meeting also might fall through the cracks as other things come up.

✓ ✓ ✓

363. Audio record all meetings. An audio recording comes in handy if someone is unable to attend the meeting and if those who did attend want to go back to a certain discussion to make sure they're on the right page. A regular audio recorder will get the job done, but you can also use the Otter Voice Notes app to create a written transcript of your meeting in real time that can be shared with attendees and others. Otter also has a search function, so you can pull up a specific part of the conversation in a snap.

364. **Make sure any necessary equipment works ahead of time.** Nothing slows down a meeting quite like faulty equipment. If you're a decision-maker when it comes to purchasing office equipment, ensure that you have what you need to get the job done right. Speakerphones, in particular, are something you want to invest in. While a regular office phone has a speaker function, it's not designed for a conference room situation. So not only will you find it hard to hear any remote attendees on the phone, but those callers probably won't be able to hear you either.

365. **Be clear about your meeting goals and why you need a specific attendee there.** People who know they've been *personally* selected to be part of a group are much more likely to arrive on time with good ideas in tow than those who feel they were haphazardly added to an invite list. The same goes for assigning tasks in those meetings. Make sure your assignee knows why he was chosen. If you can't be clear about why something is important and why you chose that person, then he won't understand its importance either.

366. **Limit phone meetings to just a few people.** Phone meetings are complicated and rarely worth it with more than a few attendees. Inevitably someone speaking in the room will be far enough away from the speakerphone that he can't be heard by those calling in. If what the person said is important (and it should be if it's being said in the meeting), then you'll need to waste time by repeating it again closer to the phone so others can hear. Never have a phone meeting where there's a conference room full of people.

✓ ✓ ✓

367. **Choose which items you're willing to ditch from your agenda if time starts running out.** Ideally, you'll be able to hit every topic you plan on, but if time runs short, you want to have an idea of what items can be moved to a later discussion. When you don't have a plan, you run the risk of losing the time you needed for an important item to a less-important item.

3 6 8 . **Keep PowerPoint presentations short and simple.** By and large, creating elaborate PowerPoint presentations is more trouble than it's worth, and people often use these slides (usually full of useless content) as a crutch in public speaking. If you want to use PowerPoint in your meeting, limit the information you put on each slide to just a few data points or a single graph or picture. Making the presentation will take you a lot less time this way, and during the meeting you'll be able to focus more on talking to people rather than reading through long, complicated slides.

✓ ✓ ✓

3 6 9 . **Mix things up.** Too much of any one thing will leave people bored and unengaged in your meeting. Change things up between presentations, smaller group discussions, and any sort of physical activity. The more variety you can incorporate into your meeting, the more engaged your audience will be and the better the meeting will go.

370. **Keep the meeting under an hour.** After an hour, people are going to start getting distracted (they can't help it!). If a longer meeting *is* necessary, schedule a fifteen- to twenty-minute break around that one-hour mark so people can check up on email, visit the restroom, or tend to other responsibilities. When you return to the meeting, you'll have a refreshed and newly engaged group.

371. **Email the key takeaways to everyone after the meeting.** An email can serve as a nice recap for everyone and will keep the meeting fresh in their minds—and their inboxes!

372.

Don't stick around in a long meeting if you don't have to. If your role in a meeting is simply to talk about one small aspect of a project, see if the meeting organizer is okay with you leaving the room after that portion is done. There's no reason to sit through an hour-long meeting if the part that pertains to you is just a few minutes long. A lot can get done in that extra time!

373. **Reward those who show up early.** Think of some benefit to offer the first few people who arrive at a meeting. That benefit could be something like first dibs at assignments for a new project or even a gift card to the coffee shop around the corner. Having everyone at your meeting on time will help you move through your day much faster, so reward those who are helping you get there!

374. **Keep everyone on their toes—literally.** If you want to keep a meeting brief, try having everyone remain standing. When people are standing, they are less likely to have long conversations and will instead be focused on getting things done so they can go back to their desks.

UNIQUE PLACES TO HOLD A MEETING

Conference rooms can get boring, especially if you're sitting in the same stiff chairs and looking at the same whiteboard every time you have a meeting. Picking a new location for your meeting, especially when it is a longer one, can help inspire creativity among attendees and ultimately make your meeting more productive. Here are a few ideas for new locations:

375. A picnic area near your office building.

376. At a restaurant over lunch. The relaxed atmosphere can encourage more creative thinking.

377. A coffee shop. This is a great spot for one-on-one meetings.

378. Your client's office. This is an easy change from always holding meetings in your office, and it will help them feel more comfortable.

379. A fun attraction such as a brewery or aquarium. Many places offer event space that can be booked for daylong meetings.

380. A rented space. Services such as Breather and LiquidSpace allow you to rent a charming, productivity-boosting space in minutes. The location comes fully prepared with Wi-Fi, chargers, video screens, and more.

381. A nature trail. Get those creative juices flowing by holding your next brainstorming meeting while on a hike near your office.

382. A bookstore. A large bookstore with access to Wi-Fi can be just the boost of inspiration you and your attendees need. This location is perfect for smaller meetings.

383. A spa. Many spas offer meeting rooms that are a relaxing place to discuss a topic people may be dreading. Even better, you can treat the team to a massage treatment after.

384. Happy hour. If your meeting is casual and involves just a few people (or is one-on-one), consider turning it into an early happy hour that will encourage everyone to offer their thoughts on a project.

385. **Cancel a meeting if you aren't prepared.** Having someone cancel a meeting you've blocked off on your schedule is annoying, but it's not as annoying as someone wasting your time in a meeting because she's not prepared for it. If you're not ready, save everyone the trouble and simply reschedule for a time when you are.

386. **Consider having the meeting over lunch.** A lunch meeting allows you to fuel your body while getting work done. Lunch meetings are rarely useful for large groups because you run can into issues where it is too hard to hear everyone in a restaurant or coordinate food orders for delivery, but they can be a great way to handle one-on-one conversations or small group discussions with three or four people.

CHAPTER 6

TECHNOLOGY
AND TOOLS

387. **Don't want to buy a dedicated work phone for your home office?** Google Voice gives you a special number on top of your existing number to associate with your cell phone or to forward to another phone or even your email account. With forwarding you can turn the number off and on depending on when you're available to take calls. You can also leave the number permanently "off" so it forwards calls straight to voice mail. Voice mails from Google Voice numbers are transcribed and delivered to your email so you can see what the calls were about before deciding how to handle them.

388. **Turn off social media notifications.** Save yourself from being bombarded with distracting messages from *Facebook* groups, *Instagram* posts, or *Twitter* updates by turning off those account notifications.

389. Cut down on how much time you spend aimlessly surfing the web with RescueTime. This app will track how much time you spend on certain websites and certain apps on your computer. Once you have that information about how you're using your computer, you can make informed decisions about what changes you should make. For instance, you might realize you're spending three hours on *Facebook* every day or half of your day just responding to email—so you better understand what things to avoid.

✓ ✓ ✓

390. Read distraction-free with Just Read. Web pages are meant to be distracting. Colorful fonts, videos that autoplay, and numerous ads are all trying to distract you from the article that you're reading. The Google Chrome extension Just Read will remove things like flashy web page styles, pop-up ads, and comments, and turn the article into a simplified text.

391. **Get motivation to put down your phone with Forest.** This app grows virtual trees when you're not using your phone. When you launch an app, or browse the Internet or social media on your phone, the trees wither and die. They're not real trees, but the experience will make you more cognizant of how much you're using your phone and encourage you to keep it put away so your virtual trees (and productivity) can grow.

392. **Use Hop Email for more focused group chats.** If you're stuck in a long email chain when collaborating on a project, Hop Email can transform that email conversation into a chat-style one, making the collaboration feel a bit more intuitive. The app strips out email headers, signatures, and quoted text from past emails to streamline the reading process and your workflow.

393. **Use different computers for your personal and work use.** If you have to use the same device for both, consider creating two separate profiles, one for your "work personality" and the other for your "home personality." With two profiles, you can do things like block social media websites on your work browser without impacting how you use your computer in your free time.

394. **Make sure your work is typo-free with Grammarly.** This web and mobile app can read through the text you write and look for any spelling or grammar errors. It can be a great "second set of eyes" in a pinch when you are working on a big project and need to make sure you haven't missed any errors. It also works with email and web forms so you can always put your best professional foot forward.

395. If you need to work with your coworkers on a document, keep it in a cloud service such as Dropbox, Box, or Google Drive so you all have access to it. By storing something in the cloud, you ensure that you're always working with the most recent version of a file. This saves both you and your coworkers from doubling up on work that's already been done, and it verifies that you're all on the same page—literally.

396. Break up your workday wisely by using Tide. This app helps you track your periods of work and rest, and it offers ambient sound options such as rain to help you stay focused during work periods. The app defaults to twenty-five minutes of work followed by five minutes of rest, but you can also customize settings to match your own personal work habits.

397. **Use Boomerang or Streak to schedule emails to go out at specific times.** Handling email late at night or early in the morning can make things easier since you're not dealing with an influx of emails at the same time. These apps will send out your emails whenever you choose so they won't get lost in someone's inbox.

398. **Text and send emails faster from your mobile phone using SwiftKey.** This app replaces the existing keyboard on your phone with one that learns your typing over time. It allows you to then customize the keyboard to meet your needs and make typing from your device much faster.

399. **Never lose a note again with Evernote.** This cloud-based service has been a favorite of productivity enthusiasts since its launch and can store everything from your screenplay to receipts from your business trips. You can make and store lists, take notes in a meeting, or even "clip" articles from the web to read later. Notes and notebooks can also be shared with others, just as if you were passing a physical notebook to a friend.

400. **Avoid unnecessary inbox check-ins with Checker Plus.** Keeping your email open all day can be detrimental to your productivity. If you can't entirely walk away from your inbox, this Google Chrome extension will let you know when you've received a new message without you having to constantly visit your inbox. You can also read and respond to the message right from Google Chrome.

401. **Handle multiple social media accounts at once using Buffer.** This free app supports *Twitter, Facebook, Instagram, Google+,* and *LinkedIn,* and it allows you to schedule posts on those platforms so you don't have to spend so much of your time on updates. Free users are able to schedule ten posts in a queue across three different accounts. A premium account allows you to schedule unlimited messages across all of the social networks.

✓ ✓ ✓

402. **Keep browser tabs organized with Snooze Tabby.** If you're someone who likes to leave a window open so you can visit it later, you know how easy it can be to end up with so many tabs open that you can't find anything you need. Snooze Tabby is a Google Chrome and Firefox extension that allows you to snooze tabs that you've opened and have them pop back up later when they will be needed. For instance, you can snooze the fun articles you find during your workday and have them pop back up again in your browser during lunch or after the workday is done.

403. **Do you need background noise to focus on your work?** Noisli may be just the app you need to get things done. This app allows users to create their own perfect mix of white, pink, and brown noise to make the perfect soundtrack to your workday. These colors refer to sound frequencies and their power, with white having the most range of frequency at a steady power, pink having slightly more power in its lower frequencies, and brown having even more power in its lower frequencies. Noisli's built-in timer can also help you set specific bursts of work time.

404. **Use the Gmail canned response feature to send emails that you type often.** To get to it, click the gear icon in the top right corner, and then select Settings, followed by the Advanced tab. From there, click to enable Canned Responses, then scroll down and select Save Changes. Now when you compose a new message, click on the three dots on the lower right side of the window and select Canned responses. From the resulting menu you can save a new canned response or access the ones you've already saved.

405. **Set up chain reactions with IFTTT (If This Then That).** This web service can dramatically enhance your productivity by creating situations where if one thing happens, another thing happens as well. The service works with a host of different websites, apps, and smart home devices, and it allows you to create "recipes" where a chain reaction will occur. These "recipes" can be simple, like always posting your *Twitter* tweets to *Facebook*, or more complex, like turning your house lights off when you start your car.

✓ ✓ ✓

406. **Don't waste time printing, signing, and rescanning a form.** HelloSign allows you to sign documents right on your computer so you can skip those printing and scanning steps.

ESSENTIAL MAC KEYBOARD SHORTCUTS

Keyboard shortcuts will make you much more efficient when it comes to working on your computer. Here are a few essentials worth learning if you use a Mac:

407. Pressing Command + W will close the window that you're currently browsing in. You can close all of the active browser windows by pressing Option + Command + W.

408. If you're using an app and you want to look at its Preferences menu, you can get there by pressing Command + ,.

409. If you need to find something on your computer, pressing Command + space bar will bring up Spotlight, where you can type in a search query. You can also ask Siri by pressing and holding Command + space bar.

410. If you'd rather speak than type, press the Fn button twice to launch Dictation. You'll need to enable the feature the first time you use it.

411. If you press the X button on the top left corner of an application window, you'll close the window but not the app. If you want to shut the app down completely, press Command + Q.

412. You can find a word on a web page or a song in your iTunes library by pressing Command + F. This will launch a small search window where you can type in what you're looking for.

413. Force quit an application that's misbehaving by pressing Command + Option + Esc.

414. Take a screenshot of your entire page by pressing Command + Shift + 3. If you want a screenshot of just a portion of the screen, press Command + Shift + 4. A small set of crosshairs will appear that you can use to draw a box over the area you want to capture.

415. Feeling distracted? Pressing Command + Option + H will hide all of the other apps on your computer except the one you're currently using so you can focus on your work.

416. Quickly navigate to the Applications and Utilities folders by pressing Command + Shift + A for applications, and Command + Shift + U for utilities.

417. **Filter your emails with Astro.** Astro is an AI-powered assistant that works with Gmail and Office 365 email addresses. The app prioritizes emails that it thinks are important for you to read and highlights ones you can probably ignore. For instance, if you get a promotional email from a store every week that you never open, Astro may suggest that it's time to unsubscribe. If you use the service regularly, it can be a powerful tool in finally getting (and keeping) an empty inbox.

418. **Set the software on your mobile phone and computer to update automatically.** Computer and phone companies routinely put out small updates that fix bugs and patch up security issues. When you don't download the updates, you can make your devices vulnerable to hackers. Save time—and your software—with automatic updates.

419.

Invest in a Smart Lock. Beyond the ease of being able to unlock your home with your phone, a Smart Lock allows you to grant others access to your home for short periods of time as well. For instance, you might give a houseguest a code for your home that works only for the weekend, or you might open the door remotely for a delivery person so he can drop off a package, saving you a trip to the post office later in the day to pick up what you missed.

420. **Switch your phone's coloring to grayscale.**
When your phone is in black and white, all of the app icons will look similar, and they'll be less likely to grab your attention. For instance, when you go to check email on your phone, the colorful *Instagram* icon that would usually capture your attention and lure you in is now muted with grayscale.

421. **Have a tablet collecting dust on your desk?**
Consider using it as a second monitor with your computer. You probably don't want to have it handle a lot of heavy lifting, but it can be useful for keeping your inbox open or your calendar running and accessible during the day. For things like email and calendars you can just run a calendar or email app on the tablet directly. If you have an iPad and want to make it a true second monitor, you can do that with the paid app Duet Display.

422. **Regularly back up the contents of your mobile devices to your cloud service.** Accidents happen. You can easily leave your smartphone in a cab or accidentally drop it and lose it forever. If you have everything backed up, then even if your laptop gets stolen or your phone accidentally takes a swim in the pool, you'll still have access to all of the content that was stored on it. You can then get a replacement and be back online with a duplicate of your original device just minutes after you leave the store.

423. **Build good habits with HabitHub.** This app has a built-in calendar where you can monitor your habit "streak" as well as a reminder system to help keep you on track. It also has a journaling application so you can keep notes on your progress. If you have a smartwatch, you can receive reminders on your wrist.

424. **Download SitOrSquat to save your time—and your bladder.** Sometimes we all need to use a public restroom. If you happen to be in a shop with a restroom, then you're in the clear. However, if you're walking around and there's no bathroom in sight, you can waste a lot of time looking for somewhere open to the public that you can go. The app SitOrSquat is loaded with over 100,000 restroom locations. Even better, it has photos of a lot of these restrooms as well as ratings from previous guests to give you an idea of what you're in for when you arrive.

☑ ☑ ☑

425. **Stay in touch when you travel with WhatsApp.** This app is tied to your phone number but doesn't need a cell signal to work. Instead it sends messages (for free) to your contacts over Wi-Fi. That means that if you're traveling with a few folks who don't want to spring for the international data plan, you can still send messages to each other.

426. **Control your website access with StayFocusd.** This Google Chrome extension allows you to set time limits for certain websites and makes those websites temporarily unavailable when your time is up. The idea is that you can still have some access to the website during the day, but you won't be able to fall into a time-sucking web browsing session.

✓ ✓ ✓

427. **Get a smart thermostat.** This app-controlled thermostat will prevent you from having to constantly adjust the temperature in your home, and it can help you keep your energy bills low. The device will learn how you use it and then make adjustments accordingly. Depending on the brand, it can also sense when you've left the house for the day and adjust the temperature to a more cost-conscious level—or realize you're playing hooky for the morning and keep the temperature comfortable for you.

428. **Don't waste time looking for your keys.** Tile is an app that offers small Bluetooth fobs that you can attach to your keys (or anything else you might misplace) and pair with your mobile phone. Now if you can't find your keys in the morning, you can ping them from your phone and have them make a noise so you can find them quickly, instead of spending twenty minutes of your morning tearing apart the couch.

429. **Use Google Translate.** This app translates between two chosen languages. It also has an image feature for many languages that can translate words from a photo, like one of a street sign or menu. In addition, it lets you save phrases and sentences ahead of time—so you don't end up frantically typing to ask someone a question when you're in a hurry. Before you travel, make sure you download the native language for your destination so you will have access to the service even when you don't have a data connection.

430. **Supercharge your work lists with Trello.** This web service allows you to create virtual lists that are made out of individual cards. Cards can be dragged and dropped from one list to another as well as loaded with information, photos, and even their own sublists. For projects with lots of moving parts, Trello is a quick and easy way to stay organized. You can even make lists available to your entire team, and the mobile app will keep you connected to those lists even when you're away from your computer.

☑ ☑ ☑

431. **Don't waste your valuable lunch meeting time waiting for a table.** OpenTable has long been the front-runner in the reservation space and can allow you to make a reservation for dinner or even find a place to go based on your location. Yelp also offers reservations, as do the apps Resy and Nowait. Before heading out for a meal, check one of those and see if you can book a table so it's ready to go when you arrive.

432. **Add a period to your Gmail address to filter unwanted emails.** For instance, you can give your close friends jane.doe@gmail.com as your email address and give others janedoe@gmail.com. Both emails will still be recognized as yours, but you can filter messages by the address the sender used, allowing you to focus on the emails that matter rather than having to wade through emails that don't.

433. **Stay on top of your finances using Mint.** Made by the creators of TurboTax, this app connects to your credit cards and bank accounts and then puts all your financial information in one place. By keeping your finances together and organized during the year, the app makes doing your taxes (and staying on budget) a breeze.

434. **Use a digital assistant to remind you of important tasks.** For instance, if you're in the middle of something right now but want to make sure you place a phone call by three p.m., ask Alexa or Siri to remind you to make the call at two forty-five p.m. Setting the reminder is easy, and it can be just the nudge you need later when your mind is focused on other things.

✔ ✔ ✔

435. **Save time by adopting a company chat product.** Services like Slack can help get all of your team members, no matter where they are, in the same virtual workspace. There you can create different chat rooms to discuss individual projects as well as send direct messages to colleagues to ask quick questions rather than calling or sending an email. By keeping all your work conversations in the same place, you can streamline your workflow and make work, in general, a lot easier. Even better, all those conversations are searchable later in case you forget what was discussed or need a refresher on some of the finer points.

436. **Download audio content onto your phone.**
Apps like Audible are great for downloading
entire books you can listen to when you're
walking or commuting. Educational podcasts
are also a great choice to have on hand and
can allow you to learn something new during
your travels rather than just sleep or veg out.

437. **Skip ATMs and IOUs with an app like Square or
Venmo.** These apps let you send someone money instantly using your phone—no need to break
large bills or figure out where the nearest ATM is.

438. **Try turning off Wi-Fi to fully disconnect from your computer at night.** You can use your router's parental controls to turn the Wi-Fi off in your home at a specific time, like an hour before bed. Yes, since it's your router you could just turn it on again, but the disconnection forces you to think about how late it is and how you could be focusing on something more productive instead.

☑ ☑ ☑

439. **Use HazeOver to "dim" distracting desktop tasks.** HazeOver dims everything in the background of the app you're working on. In dimming everything else, your current work is highlighted on the screen, capturing (and keeping) your attention. It's not quite as effective as just closing all your other windows, but if you're in a situation where you need to leave things open, it can make focusing easier.

ESSENTIAL WINDOWS KEYBOARD SHORTCUTS

Keyboard shortcuts are a simple way to navigate your computer tasks in record time. The following are a few essential shortcuts for every Windows user:

440. Press Windows + PrtScn to capture a screenshot of your entire computer screen.

441. Switch between two open apps on your computer by pressing Alt + Tab.

442. Press Windows + L to lock your computer if you need to walk away for a few minutes. This will keep anyone else from accessing your computer while you're gone.

443. Press Control + A to select all of the text on a current page.

444. If you need to get to something on your home screen but you have a lot of windows open, press Windows + D to quickly minimize all of the open windows on your screen and bring your home screen into view.

445. Refresh a web page by pressing F5.

446. Search for files on your computer by pressing Windows + S. From the search box, you'll be able to type in a query or ask Cortana. If you want to speak to her specifically, you can launch Cortana by pressing Windows + C.

447. Close an app on your computer by pressing Alt + F4.

448. Press Windows + = to zoom in on the page or app you're currently viewing. When you're done, you can press Windows + - to zoom out.

449. Rename a file by highlighting its name and then pressing F2.

450. **Combine your calendar and your to-do list with Sunsama.** Described as "if Trello and Google Calendar had a baby," this app allows you to create to-do lists that are tied to a calendar. One huge benefit of the service is you can add tasks to your to-do list weeks or months in advance that you know need to be handled on a specific day. Tasks can also be prioritized in the app.

451. **Cut down on cleaning with a robot vacuum.** A Roomba will learn your home's layout and vacuum things up on a schedule that you set. You'll still need to clean, but the robot can keep things at least a little tidier during busy weeks.

452. **Never forget a contact again with the Accompany app.** When you work for a large company, learning everyone's name can be a pretty daunting task. Accompany is a free app that meshes together your calendar with contact management features and gives you a rundown on the people you're about to have a meeting with, what they look like (so you know who's who), and when you've communicated with them in the past. That way you can remember you worked with Erin briefly on a project five years ago, even though you may have never met her face-to-face before this meeting.

453. **Download Dayuse for a temporary office or relaxation space.** If you're on a business trip or even in your hometown and need a space to relax or work for a few hours, Dayuse allows you to book hotels for the day at a discount rather than paying for the nighttime hours as well. Another app, Breather, offers more traditional office space for rent by the hour in many major cities. It can come in handy if you need to schedule a meeting but don't have your own office space to host it in.

454. **Download FollowUp to track contacts who may need a follow-up email.** FollowUp keeps track of your emails and suggests that you follow up with a recipient who hasn't responded to your last message after a set amount of time. Even better, the app allows you to set automatic follow-ups for your emails, so if a recipient hasn't responded within a specified period of time, you know to reach out again. The service also works for setting reminders to follow up with specific web pages, online conversations, and social media profiles.

455. **If you have trouble remembering to take breaks while you're working, Stretchly can help.** Available for Mac, Windows, and Linux, the app will prompt you to take a twenty-second break every ten minutes, and a five-minute break every thirty minutes you're working. The specific timing of the breaks can be customized to meet your needs and can be scaled up or down.

456. **Use FocusWriter to write without distractions.** FocusWriter is a minimalist word processing app for Windows, Mac, and Linux that forces you to focus on something you're writing by preventing you from doing other things on your computer. The app blocks programs and websites that might take your attention away from your writing, and it allows you to set timers to break up your work into sessions so you're not working too much at once.

✓ ✓ ✓

457. **Is a friend sending you distracting messages on *Facebook*?** Mute the conversation for a few minutes or an hour by choosing it in the Messenger inbox and then selecting your preferred mute timing from the drop-down menu.

458. **Get a scanner app.** Such an app can do most everything that a traditional home scanner can for a whole lot less. Both Evernote Scannable and Adobe Scan are great options and allow you to "scan" important documents by simply snapping a photo. The finished product looks like it was done with a traditional scanner rather than a phone camera. Once you've created your scan, you can email it to whoever needs it from directly within the app.

459. **Pay with your smartphone.** When you make a purchase at a participating retailer, apps like Apple Pay and Google Pay let you simply tap your phone on the register rather than pulling out your credit card to pay. Since these apps create a unique credit card number for each transaction, paying this way is actually more secure than using your plastic card. It can also save you time since you won't have to dig around in your wallet.

460.

Be a...smart smartwatch user. A smartwatch can help you stay on top of important messages while still keeping your phone tucked away. You don't want all of your notifications coming to your wrist (so distracting!), but if you set up the watch to display only messages and calls from priority contacts, you can put your phone elsewhere and enjoy life without it always by your side.

ESSENTIAL WORD SHORTCUTS

Keyboard shortcuts make you significantly more effi-cient when it comes to using your home or work com-puter. The following are some essential Word shortcuts worth having in your arsenal:

461. You can print a document from Word by pressing Control + P on a PC, or Command + P on a Mac.

462. If you want to apply formatting to your docu-ment, you can do that by highlighting the text and pressing Control (on a PC) or Command (on a Mac) + B for bold, or Control (on a PC) or Command (on a Mac) + I for italics. If you want to remove the formatting, just repeat the action.

463. Open a new document by pressing Control + N on a PC, or Command + N on a Mac.

464. You can quickly save your work by pressing Control + S on a PC, or Command + S on a Mac.

465. Increase the font size you're typing in by press-ing Control + Shift + > on a PC, or Command + Shift + > on a Mac. Decrease font size by press-ing Control + Shift + < on a PC, or Command + Shift + < on a Mac.

466. Format what you've typed in all capital letters by pressing Control + Shift + A on a PC, or Command + Shift + A on a Mac.

467. Insert a hyperlink into your work by pressing Control + K on a PC, or Command + K on a Mac.

468. If you're not sure how to spell a word, you can launch the spell-checker by pressing F7 on a PC, or Command + Option + L on a Mac.

469. To launch Word's built-in thesaurus for a little inspiration, press Shift + F7 on a PC, or Fn + Shift + F7 on a Mac.

470. Insert a comment into your work by pressing Alt + C on a PC, or Command + Option + A on a Mac.

CHAPTER 7

MAINTAINING A WORK/LIFE BALANCE

471. **Get up early.** If you have to be at the office at nine a.m., then try to get up early enough that you have the opportunity to spend a few hours handling personal tasks before you leave. By accomplishing personal tasks ahead of time, it will be much easier to focus on your work while you're at the office, and you'll be able to do more of what you want once you're off work for the day.

472. **Airplane mode isn't just for airplanes.** Texts and phone calls can be *very* distracting. When you're at home trying to relax or focus on a personal project, turn on your device's airplane mode. Airplane mode will enable you to really tune out all that "noise" so you can enjoy that family meal or focus on that gym workout.

473. **Optimize your time at the gym with a fitness trainer or training app.** Productivity doesn't end at your home and office! Just going to the gym without a plan can result in not working out to your full potential. When you work with a trainer, she can help you build a schedule that works for you and your fitness goals, and help you achieve those goals faster than you might on your own. The same goes for a fitness app; such an app can help you build a self-guided gym regimen where you're getting the most out of every workout.

☑ ☑ ☑

474. **Keep work-related chat and email apps off your phone!** If you always have work with you, you're never going to feel like you've truly left the office. That means while everyone else is enjoying their evening and coming back refreshed in the morning, you're not getting the benefit of the break and may come back already burned out. Keep work at work and home at home; you'll be better off in both places when you do.

STEPS TO CREATING THE PERFECT DAILY TO-DO LIST

You may think creating a to-do list is as easy as jotting down each thing you want to accomplish that day. However, many people can run into the issue of either creating so many to-do items that they become overwhelmed, or combining actions into much larger to-dos that leave them wondering where to start. Fear not! Here are a few simple tips for becoming a list-making pro:

475. Have a different to-do list for each day to target that day's specific needs.

476. Make sure every item is something you can *realistically* do that day.

477. Create a mix of both personal and professional daily goals for your list.

478. Break large items into smaller tasks.

479. Make sure every action item is as specific as possible. When you know exactly what needs to happen, you won't accidentally overlook a portion of a project or misinterpret your own notes.

480. Include everything you need to do in a day, even the small stuff like mailing bills or filling up your gas tank.

481. Divide your list into things that have to get done today and things that you'd like to do if you have time.

482. Make sure your list includes even easy items (like taking out the trash) to keep you motivated. When you feel like you're accomplishing things on your list, you'll be motivated to keep going!

483. Add phone numbers to the list for people you need to call so you don't need to hunt down the numbers when it's time to tackle that task.

484. Avoid adding so many items to your to-do list that you can't possibly finish them all.

485. **An energizing playlist isn't only for the gym.** Create a playlist of some of your favorite tunes to play whenever you really need to focus on a task and get things done quickly. Upbeat music can be the perfect soundtrack not only for running on the treadmill but also for cleaning your kitchen, packing for a big trip, or organizing your files. Find some music that gives you energy, and then break it out whenever you're starting to fall into a slump.

486. **Adjust your schedule so you do errands before or after the crowds arrive.** Why go grocery shopping on Sunday afternoon when you know you'll be stuck with empty shelves and long lines? Instead, if you go during less popular hours, you'll be able to maneuver through the store or gym a little easier, and you won't waste time standing in line or navigating the packed parking lot. Even if you're able to save only fifteen minutes each week, that will still add up to an extra hour of time to do something else (or relax) at the end of the month.

487. **Avoid double-booking by keeping a digital version of your family calendar.** Everyone can add activities to it, and it will also guarantee that everyone knows what the plan is for the week. Knowing that your spouse is in a meeting until six or that your child has rehearsal for the school play until seven will help you plan your day better.

488. **Don't be afraid to delegate responsibilities in your personal life.** For instance, maybe your thirteen-year-old can be in charge of keeping the guest bathroom clean, and your eleven-year-old can make sure the dog goes out every morning and evening. Everyone should have their own tasks that they're responsible for.

489. **Use the freezer!** Things like soups and chili are easy to prep and then freeze to cook later. If you have enough freezer space, keep a few meals in your freezer at all times just in case. For instance, the next time you make chili, try prepping double the amount and freezing half. A few months later when you're having a particularly busy week, you can throw that already prepped chili into the slow cooker one morning and have dinner ready when you get home that night.

490. **"No" isn't always a bad word.** One key to being your most productive is knowing your limits and giving yourself adequate time to tend to the task at hand without getting bogged down by things you don't need to do. If you're working on a huge project and some friends invite you over for dinner, you might want to say yes, but you'll be much better off saying no.

491.

Have some goals in mind before you head to the gym. Wandering around the gym aimlessly from machine to machine is time-consuming and can slow down the flow of your workout. Instead, go in with a plan such as doing cardio for thirty minutes and then working on your arms. You might have to change things up when you're there based on equipment availability, but having a plan will help you focus your efforts from the get-go so you can get a good workout in.

492. **Smile more.** Studies have proven that smiling can reduce both your stress and anxiety levels. If you're starting to feel a little burned out, take a minute to watch a funny video or look at funny pictures. Stress can slow you down, make you less efficient at your work, and even lead to illness (which will definitely leave you down for the count). Stay cool, calm, and collected during the day to be your most productive self.

493. **Write your own monthly or annual reviews.** By writing a "review" just as if being you was a job position, you force yourself to look at what you've done well during the month and what parts of your life need improvement. When you reflect back on the month (or year), you might notice that you've put off your physical health and need to incorporate more exercise into your schedule. Or maybe you haven't put as much time into a project as you should have. By reflecting on the past, you can set yourself up for a more productive future.

494. **Is there a point in your day when you always find yourself least productive?** Turn that into your gym time. Heading to the gym will be a break from what you're working on, and it will get your heart and blood pumping to rejuvenate you for the remainder of the day. If you work in an office, you might not be able to go right when you hit that slump, but the closer you can get to it, the better. If you can't make it to the gym, consider a small break to do a few stretches at your desk. Using an exercise ball in place of a chair can also break things up during your day and give your body a little change of pace.

✓ ✓ ✓

495. **Try a laundry service.** Laundry is one of the most time-consuming (and dreaded) tasks out there. Once you put your clothes in the wash, you're tethered to the washer—and then the dryer after that—or you run the risk of wrinkled or shrunken clothes. If you can, have a company do your laundry. Once it's off your plate, you'll be surprised at how much more time you have in your week.

496.

Take one small step toward a long-term goal each day. For instance, if your goal is to become fluent in French, learn five new words a day. If you want to be a better writer, write for fifteen minutes every morning or evening. Doing something small each day for even just a few minutes will get you that much closer to a big goal. If you learned just five new French words a day, you'd know over 1,800 words by the end of the year.

497. **Create a meal plan for the week.** Meal plans should include everything from breakfast to dinner. Knowing what the plan is for each day guarantees that you get everything you need in a single trip to the grocery store and that you're not sitting around on a Wednesday night trying to figure out what's for dinner. If there are a few foods you or your family love, set specific days for those foods. For instance, you might have "Taco Tuesday" and "Pizza Friday."

498. **Take the time to be nice to people you meet and to express gratitude to those who help you.** Nice things come to nice people. People who feel appreciated will be much more likely to help you out in the future than those who don't. And to be your most productive self, you're going to need the help of others!

499. **Bring friends.** Doing something with friends can dramatically improve how you feel about that task. Even painting the fence can be a good time with the right group of people. Try to involve your friends in as much of your life as possible. When you have friends there, you'll have a much better experience.

500. **Set quarterly "purge days" to keep your home decluttered.** When you live in a mess, things are hard to find and you're more stressed out. Use these scheduled purge days to do a deep clean of your home and donate unused items to a thrift store. When you regularly purge your home of items you no longer use, maintaining a clean home will be easier—as will finding things.

501. **Give yourself a night off at least once a week to kick back and relax without a schedule.** You'll start the next day more refreshed, and you'll likely be much more productive than you would have been had you worked through the night.

502. **Speed things up.** Listening to podcasts and books on tape can be both educational and entertaining, but they can also take up a ton of time. Whenever you listen to something that's prerecorded, consider bumping the speed up to at least 1.25. You don't want to make the recording so fast that you can't understand what you're listening to, but a slightly faster speed will allow you to plow through significantly more material in less time.

503. **Choose a gym near your home or office.** If you select a gym that's difficult for you to get to, then chances are you just won't go. Picking a nearby location will cut down on your commute time to go work out and guarantees that you go more often. It's a lot harder to make excuses for why you didn't go to the gym when you drive past it every day.

504. **If you're a parent, talk to other parents in your neighborhood about splitting up responsibilities.** For instance, maybe you pick kids up from soccer practice on Tuesdays, but another parent shuttles everyone to dance class on Saturdays. There's no reason for you both to play chauffeur at the same time when you're traveling a similar route. By sharing responsibilities, you can take some of the work off both of your plates.

505. **Use your commute time to your advantage.** If you're driving, use the time to listen to educational podcasts or to learn a new language that will help you advance in your career. If you're taking a subway or another mode of transportation where you're a passenger, consider using the time to read through reports or respond to email. By off-loading those tasks during your commute, you can make better use of your time at the office and have less to do when you get home.

506. **Consider hiring a cleaning service.** Yes, you are capable of cleaning your own dishes and bathroom, but those things take time—time that might be better spent at the gym, finally setting up the backyard grill, or spending time with your family. A cleaning service can come to your home every week or every other week to help you maintain a level of cleanliness and organization. Even having someone come just once a month to deep-clean your bathroom will give you a few valuable hours back, manage stress, and keep your home from becoming a disaster zone.

507. **Wear a fitness tracker.** A fitness tracker can help you stay on track with your fitness goals by recording what you've accomplished that day. Many trackers can also let you know when you've been sedentary for too long during the day. And while getting up every hour is great for your health, it is also great for your focus so you can come back to whatever you're working on with a new perspective and more energy.

508. **When facing a difficult task, ask someone with more experience to chip in.** For instance, putting together an IKEA bookcase is *technically* something you can do yourself, but there's a good chance you're going to get confused a few times in the process. Instead, call a friend who recently tackled a similar IKEA project and ask her to come over and build it with you (and perhaps drink a bottle of wine in the process). You'll get to see your friend, and her experience with the bookcase will make the entire process move faster.

509. **Know your strengths and play to them.** If you're great at finding errors when proofreading, then volunteer to handle those tasks. When you're working on something that you feel you're particularly good at, you'll be more motivated to get those tasks done—and done well.

510. **Simplify your closet.** Some of the most success-ful people out there have the simplest ward-robes; think about Steve Jobs's turtleneck and Mark Zuckerberg's hoodie. Streamlining your wardrobe doesn't necessarily mean sticking to a specific wardrobe piece, though: Figure out what works for you so you can take the guess-work out of planning your outfit for the next day. For instance, if you really love a particular dress shirt or pair of pants, consider buying yourself a few of them in varying colors. The goal is to cut down on planning an outfit so you can focus more of your energy and efforts on other things.

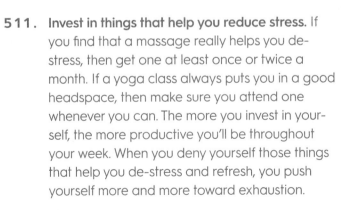

511. **Invest in things that help you reduce stress.** If you find that a massage really helps you de-stress, then get one at least once or twice a month. If a yoga class always puts you in a good headspace, then make sure you attend one whenever you can. The more you invest in your-self, the more productive you'll be throughout your week. When you deny yourself those things that help you de-stress and refresh, you push yourself more and more toward exhaustion.

512. **Always arrive at appointments and events five to ten minutes before they actually start.** When you're late, you affect everyone's productivity. Arriving five minutes early will mean you're ready to go when it's time for that meeting or appointment.

513. **Set a timer on your phone when you start browsing social media sites and using other "unnecessary" apps.** When the timer goes off, stop what you're doing and put the phone away. When you set an end time for your recreational phone use, you avoid getting sucked in and wasting hours looking at pictures on *Instagram* or finding old classmates on *Facebook*. The easiest way to curb unproductive phone use isn't to go cold turkey but to set reasonable limits for yourself.

514. **Keep a list of things that you *don't* want to do.** Having a list of things that you want to avoid is a simple way to remind yourself to cut back on those things. Things that are wasting your time and sabotaging your productivity belong on this list.

515. **Make it more convenient to balance your work and social lives by choosing the right home.** Sometimes it's harder to choose where you live, but try to select a place that is not only convenient for work but also great for the social activities you'd like to participate in. Living near the office is great for your work productivity, but if you are an hour away from the things you enjoy in your personal time, chances are your social life will suffer. Try to find a place where you're close enough to both work *and* fun.

TIPS FOR A PRODUCTIVE NIGHT'S SLEEP

Getting a good night's sleep is one of the best things you can do to boost your productivity. When you're well rested, you're more awake and alert at work. If you're having trouble falling asleep quickly, these tips can help:

516. If your mind is overworked with things you need to do, write down everything on a pad of paper to help clear your brain and remind you of those things in the morning.

517. Ditch the clock. If you have an alarm clock by your bedside table, position it so you can't see the time from bed. Counting down the minutes while you're trying to fall asleep typically makes you stay awake longer, not fall asleep faster.

518. Shower before bed. Many of us are used to showering in the morning, but taking a warm shower at night can relax your muscles and prep you for sleep.

519. Try wearing socks. Science has proven that warm hands and feet can facilitate sleep.

520. Count sheep. It actually works! Make sure to picture the physical sheep as you slowly count them. The more you count, the harder it will be to remember why you're still awake.

521. Spray your pillow with lavender before you settle in. This oil has been shown to help people relax and fall asleep faster.

522. Use a white noise machine. If you always go to bed to the sounds of a babbling brook or static from the machine, your body will learn that when it hears that noise, it's time for bed. As a bonus, the machine can drown out outside noises from your neighbors or other people in your home that might keep you awake.

523. Keep the lights low in the hour before you go to bed to get your body ready for sleep mode.

524. Skip late-night snacks and meals. They can often make it difficult to sleep or wake you up throughout the night.

525. Keep your workouts to the daytime hours. If you do need to hit the gym after work, make sure you have at least four hours between when you get home and when you go to bed to give your metabolism time to slow down.

5 2 6 . **Embrace change.** It's natural to fear change, but change is going to happen, regardless of whether or not you want it to. Instead of avoiding changes, lean into them and embrace them. Be ready to roll with the punches as they happen, and alter your goals to work with that changing landscape. If you refuse change, you'll be working against the tide, which is always much harder than riding the wave.

5 2 7 . **Use a journal to get out your thoughts about the day.** When you write things down, you'll be forced to think through your feelings on a particular topic or person. This can help you clarify why someone might have made you angry or sad, which is knowledge that you can use to improve your relationship with that person and move forward from a conflict. Journaling can also help you get a new perspective on how to handle something you're working on and set yourself up for an even more productive tomorrow.

528. **Allow yourself at least one day a week to sleep without an alarm clock.** If you've had a rough workweek, your body may need a few extra hours of shut-eye to be ready to tackle the weekend. The key is giving your body the opportunity to take what it needs rather than dictating what it's allowed to have.

529. **Ask yourself whether attending an event is necessary to your life—and if it will bring you joy.** If the answer isn't yes to at least one of those questions, skip it. Too often our calendars get filled with things we think we "have to" do. Instead, politely decline the invitation by simply saying you need to focus on something else. Even if what you need to focus on is your couch, you're spending your time better than if you attended the unnecessary event.

WAYS TO HELP YOURSELF DISCONNECT FROM THE OFFICE

In this digital age, it can be hard to disconnect when you need to. These simple hacks can help you disconnect from the office when it's time to head home for the day:

530. Leave your computer at the office when you head home. Just because your laptop is portable doesn't mean it needs to come with you.

531. Don't provide your personal number to work colleagues or business contacts. When someone has only your work contact information, then he can contact you only at work.

532. Change clothes when you get home from the office to mentally help you change gears.

533. Have a ritual for when you get home that helps you transition from work mode to relax mode.

534. Put your briefcase and other work materials in a closet or somewhere else you won't see them or be reminded of them when you're at home.

535. Give yourself a reason why you "have to" leave the office at a reasonable hour, such as a fitness class or happy hour.

536. Even if you work from home sometimes, keep work out of the places you relax so you'll never associate them with "work time." For instance, your work computer should never be opened in your living room.

537. Do something where you can't use your phone or computer, like ride a bike or go on a hike.

538. If you bring your work computer home at night, leave your charger at the office. That way you'll be limited in how much work you can do since the battery might die.

539. During your commute home, listen to something fun that helps you relax. Try an audiobook or your favorite tunes—something that makes you think "fun" rather than "work."

540. **When you're meeting with someone in person, put your phone away and leave it away.** It's easy to fall into the habit of leaving your phone on the table while you're meeting with someone. You chose to meet with this person in person rather than through email, so don't give your email more attention than you're giving that person in front of you! Your email and text notifications will still be there when you're done.

541. **Take a nap.** If you're feeling particularly sluggish and just can't seem to regain your energy, take a fifteen-minute nap. A *quick* nap (not a long one!) can be rejuvenating, and even though you're losing fifteen minutes of your day, you'll come back refreshed and more focused, which will make up for the lost time. For a real pick-me-up, drink a shot of espresso before you snooze. It takes fifteen minutes for the caffeine from the drink to hit your system, so it will give you an extra boost right when you wake up from that power nap.

INDEX

ABOUT THE AUTHOR

Emily Price is a freelance journalist based in San Francisco. Her work appears regularly on *Fast Company*, *Fortune*, *Lifehacker*, and more. You can follow her on *Twitter*: @Emily.

IMPROVE YOUR LIFE—
One Hack at a Time!